Philanthropy and Education

Series Editor

Marybeth Gasman
University of Pennsylvania
Philadelphia, Pennsylvania, USA

Aim of the Series

This series highlights first-rate scholarship related to education and philanthropy, attracting the top authors writing in the field. Philanthropy is broadly defined to include time, talent, and treasure. In addition to traditional forms and definitions of philanthropy, the series highlights philanthropy in communities of color as well as philanthropy among women and LGBT communities. Books in the series focus on fundraising as it is an integral part of increasing philanthropy and has an ever-increasing market.

More information about this series at
http://www.springer.com/series/14553

Fabrice Jaumont

Unequal Partners

American Foundations and Higher Education Development in Africa

Fabrice Jaumont
New York, NY, USA

Philanthropy and Education
ISBN 978-1-137-59346-7 (Hard cover)   ISBN 978-1-137-59348-1 (eBook)
ISBN 978-1-137-59347-4 (Soft cover)
DOI 10.1057/978-1-137-59348-1

Library of Congress Control Number: 2016950202

Cover image © Alexander Spatari

Printed on acid-free paper

This Palgrave Macmillan imprint is published by Springer Nature
The registered company is Nature America Inc. New York

FOREWORD

This study is a welcome addition to the still small but growing corpus of research on American philanthropy in Africa, a sector that has yet to be fully analyzed or understood. The author, Fabrice Jaumont, examines, among other issues, the work and legacy of the consortium of seven US foundations that, over the course of 10 years, collaborated in funding higher education initiatives in Africa. As the president of one of these foundations, Carnegie Corporation of New York, I think it is worth explaining in further detail what, exactly, motivated the Corporation to accelerate its philanthropic work on the continent.

As described in *A World of Giving*, Patricia Rosenfield's excellent book outlining the Corporation's 100-year history of international funding, Carnegie Corporation has been active in Africa since the 1920s. During the tenure of my predecessor, Dr. David Hamburg, the foundation invested in a few select policy research institutions and women's organizations. I joined the Corporation in 1997, and in 2000, the Corporation joined with the Ford, MacArthur, and Rockefeller foundations to form the Partnership for Higher Education in Africa (PHEA). They were later joined by the Hewlett, Kresge, and Mellon foundations.

In the West, the cause of African higher education had been neglected for too long; the field was in need of reinvigoration through a new generation of academics and academic leadership. This was true in sub-Saharan Africa in general and in post-apartheid South Africa in particular, where many white academics had left their home institutions or were forced out, while too many of the continent's brightest were being recruited to go into new, post-liberation governments or the corporate world. These trends left university faculties and administrations with a dearth of expertise and talent. Kofi Annan, Secretary General of the United Nations, served as the primary source of inspiration for PHEA. He advised several foundation leaders about the importance of addressing the talent gap at Africa's universities. At the Corporation, two trustees in particular, Vincent Mai, a South African, and Theresa Heinz, who was raised in Mozambique, served as advocates on behalf of African higher education and encouraged us to pursue different funding collaborations. Thus began PHEA. Over the course of 10 years, this alliance raised $440 million toward the improvement of higher education in sub-Saharan Africa and, in one instance, Egypt.

While still working within their respective missions and guidelines, the seven foundations that made up PHEA—Carnegie, Ford, Hewlett, Kresge, MacArthur, Mellon, and Rockefeller—shared several common goals. For one, we all sought to work as partners with our grantee institutions, rather than as traditional donor agencies. This was in part because we wanted to ensure African universities remained independent and in charge of their respective missions, curriculums, and destinies. In addition, we wanted to encourage the universities to not only compete with one another but cooperate, too. In funding African universities, our core guidelines for PHEA were, first, to address the most urgent needs of the universities and prioritize their goals, as defined by the universities themselves. Second, we made sure that proposals enjoyed wide support, from not only university leaders but also faculties, as well as the appropriate government ministries, such as education, finance, health, and agriculture. Third, rigorous accountability was key in all funding and program decision-making. Fourth, in order to deal with the needs and management of universities, a holistic approach to funding was imperative—human resources, communications, recruitment, and management of a university also needed to be taken into consideration. Finally, we worked hard to broaden universities' international networks by providing them with partners and advisors abroad.

While collaborating with one another, each foundation adhered to its particular mission and core strengths. For Carnegie Corporation, we realized that we could not neglect the humanities in our funding efforts. Many funders were focusing on the fields of science and technology, and even the social sciences, but the humanities were an orphan in African academia. At the urging of several African university vice chancellors, the Corporation established a major fellowship program for African scholars in the humanities, administered by the American Council of Learned Societies. We also focused on women's issues in academia—equity, fair representation, and preventing loss of talent—by introducing programs that have awarded more than 7000 full and partial scholarships to women in South Africa, Tanzania, Uganda, Ghana, and Nigeria. In addition, following in the Corporation's long-standing tradition of supporting libraries, we helped several African universities establish research commons, and also funded major public libraries in South Africa, including the national library in Pretoria and libraries in Johannesburg and Cape Town, as well as a model children's library in Pietermaritzburg. A model branch library in Khayelitsha, a Cape Town township, rounded out the Corporation's public library investments. Our efforts were not confined to libraries and higher education institutions, however. We also launched a major program called the Regional Initiative in Science and Education (RISE), which trained a new generation of scientists with the aim of combating "brain drain" at African universities through promoting cross-regional collaboration among African scientists, universities, and laboratories.

Though PHEA met with great success in many areas, it faced a number of challenges along the way. One was the issue of language. Africa is home to four major colonial languages—English, French, Portuguese, and Arabic—in addition to hundreds of African language groups and dialects. The partner foundations ultimately decided to work primarily in Anglophone countries, and particularly in South Africa, due to preexisting investments in those regions. For example, Carnegie Corporation's charter authorized us to invest up to 7.4% of our funds abroad, but only in British Dominion, hence Anglophone, countries. However, PHEA did work in Mozambique (where the official language is Portuguese) as the Ford and Rockefeller foundations were already active there. Similarly, Egypt and Madagascar were later added to the list of PHEA countries due to the long-standing and emergent interests of several PHEA foundations in those areas.

After settling on target languages and regions, another challenge the PHEA foundations encountered was balancing their sometimes-divergent priorities. As mentioned earlier, each foundation decided to be, as much as possible, faithful to its mission and goals throughout the 10-year collaborative. Doing so, however, meant that at times PHEA struggled to develop and maintain unifying, overarching themes in its funding. For example, while Carnegie Corporation was intent on assisting some of the most promising universities and supporting the emergence of new scholars and scientists, other foundations' investments were farther afield. The Rockefeller Foundation, for one, was heavily invested in agriculture and public health, and much, though not all, of its contributions within PHEA reflected those priorities. Similarly, while the MacArthur Foundation's program in Nigeria looked much like Carnegie Corporation's, many of its additional investments in African higher education reflected the foundation's emphasis on conservation. Meanwhile, the Ford Foundation's PHEA investments in Mozambique and elsewhere were diverse and multi-faceted. They ranged from institutional strengthening at Eduardo Mondlane University and, later, Catholic University in Mozambique to pipeline studies in East and West Africa, which aimed to provide greater university admission opportunities for poor students.

This being said, PHEA foundations found innovative and important ways to collaborate. For example, the partnership agreed to collectively fund the Bandwidth Consortium, a $5.5 million investment that ultimately lowered bandwidth costs for participating African universities by as much as 300%. The effort was born out of a consensus reached at a PHEA gathering of foundation officers and African academics, librarians, and technologists. Ultimately, PHEA investments reflected new and ongoing foundation priorities. During the last 5 years of the partnership, the foundations collaborated much more closely.

Finally, one major concern PHEA worked hard to allay was that, in light of the partnership's investments, African governments would reduce their contributions to higher education. Ultimately, however, this concern proved unfounded—the governments remained faithful to their promise not to reduce their funding commitments to universities. Today, government remains African higher education's primary funder. The PHEA foundations were also pleased that we were able to work directly with African universities and research institutions rather than through governments, unlike international aid agencies, such as the US Agency for International Development, the World Bank, and the African Development Bank, though the partnership made sure to involve government officials whenever possible. In doing so, we provided universities additional autonomy. Our positive experiences also encouraged several European foundations to follow our line of grantmaking in African higher education.

When PHEA concluded in 2010, we were proud of a number of successes. For one, over the course of the partnership's 10 years, African university leadership had come to appreciate the necessity of maintaining strong registrar's offices, alumni offices, and communications departments, as well as the importance of first-rate research commons. PHEA was also instrumental in establishing the *Journal of Higher Education in Africa* and a news site, University World News: Africa Edition, which are tasked with covering developments in the field for the entire continent. We helped broaden the universities' fundraising abilities, and also made connections between a large swath of university leadership and learned societies, not just among African institutions, but with peers in Europe and the USA. Finally, PHEA activities helped increase opportunities for female students, academics, and university administrators. In a sense, the partnership exposed African universities to higher education practices in other countries, which aided in the African higher education system's overall modernization. Perhaps most importantly, PHEA's work underscored the need for strong universities in Africa. It is a cause that the World Bank and other international organizations have since taken up. Before, many had seen K-12 education as the top priority, but no longer—players across Africa and around the world now recognize higher education as central to Africa's development.

Carnegie Corporation is among the many international agencies, governments, and foundations that have continued to support African higher education since the partnership ended in 2010. We have maintained our humanities fellowships and scholarships programs, and also launched initiatives addressing the diaspora of African academics. These programs encourage African academics to earn their PhDs at African universities rather than going abroad, and also work to bring expatriate academics back to the continent in order to establish stronger linkages between universities and develop and strengthen African faculties.

The new support for African higher education is perhaps best reflected in the continent-wide summit, "Revitalizing Higher Education for Africa's Future," held in Dakar, Senegal, in March 2015. The event, which brought together education and civil leaders from all over Africa and the globe, resulted in a declaration and action plan drafted and endorsed by African participants and later tabled at a meeting of the African Union. While PHEA can claim to have made a demonstrable contribution to African higher education, it is the continuing advocacy of African higher education leaders and the commitment of their governments that will determine the future of higher education on the continent.

It is our hope that PHEA's experiences, chronicled and analyzed in this text, will prove useful and provide some guidance to governments and international organizations interested in making philanthropic investments in African higher education, particularly in non-Anglophone countries. It is a cause that deserves investment—PHEA should not be considered an end, but a beginning and, we hope, an inspiration to those in the philanthropy, education, and development fields.

Carnegie Corporation of New York   Vartan Gregorian
New York, NY, USA

Series Editor Preface

Fabrice Jaumont has written a book that needed to be written decades ago. *Unequal Partners: American Foundations and Higher Education Development in Africa* tells the complicated story of how philanthropy has shaped higher education, in both positive and negative ways. Although the "great" philanthropists have been lauded in many books for decades, recent scholarship has challenged their benevolence and that of their foundations. Jaumont provides a fair portrayal of major foundation players in African higher education—those with a long track record and those that have just started to play a role. Rather than present these foundations as saviors that uplift higher education on the continent, Jaumont presents a nuanced view, detailing the profound impact as well as the "unequal" relationships that result when one of the partners has more resources and the other is in need of resources. Of note, the discussions and themes featured in the book are useful to those studying and working with foundations in the USA as well as in Africa. Interestingly, many of the interventions in Africa are similar to those in urban and minority communities in the USA. Overall, *Unequal Partners* is beautifully written, succinctly and effectively argued, and timely.

University of Pennsylvania   Marybeth Gasman
Philadelphia, PA, USA

PREFACE

The goal of this book is to explore the relationship between US private foundations and universities in Africa. Nearly 100 US private foundations are active in the field of African higher education, while many more make regular grants to other fields in Africa. All grants combined, these foundations collectively contributed an unprecedented $4 billion between 2003 and 2013 to support Africa through projects run either by Africa-based institutions or by intermediaries such as non-governmental agencies and institutions based in developed countries. Findings show that in a 10-year period, cumulative grants to Africa have increased steadily in size and in quantity; grant distribution per sector shows a larger concentration in health, education, and international development; and geographic grant distribution shows a major concentration in Commonwealth countries.

As American foundations are focusing more and more attention on issues of international interest, turning their attention to problems that cross borders and that are produced by globalization processes, it has become critical to assess their funding trends, as well as their ideological background and influence over niche sectors such as African higher education. African universities have received funding from US private foundations for almost a century, with a significant increase in grants and grant amounts since 2000. It is hard to determine whether or not the initiatives that US private foundations sponsor in African universities have had an influence over their development. That said, in educational philanthropy, one needs only to look at the history of foundation work to recognize that US foundations have never been neutral; moreover, they have traditionally provided substantive direction and have exerted significant authority over educational policy. Through their longevity and accumulated expertise in African education, The Rockefeller Foundation, Ford Foundation, and Carnegie Corporation of New York, for instance, have significantly infused their grantees' development with a *Western* perspective, particularly through the Africanization and modernization phases of the 1960s and 1970s, when the human capital theory, which viewed higher education as an important investment for societies, was prevalent among educational policy-makers.

Funding to higher education is dependent on both national and global shifts in the grantors' country, and in the receptiveness of African governments and institutions to the modalities of private funding. Today, neo-liberal trends have promoted the notion of the knowledge economy, which sees higher education as crucial for economic growth. The emergence of newer foundations, such as The Andrew W. Mellon Foundation, John D. and Catherine T. MacArthur Foundation, The William and Flora Hewlett Foundation, Charles Stewart Mott Foundation, W. K. Kellogg Foundation, and The Kresge Foundation, which invest in the sector of African higher education, is regenerating entire academic networks on the African continent after a 20-year lull that ended in 2000. These foundations promote interconnectedness and internationalization, assisting a handful of African universities into the twenty-first century, and leading many others into a competition for which they might not yet be ready.

With this in mind, it is important to understand the role played by foundations, particularly those that seek to impact fields such as health, culture, education, public policy, economic development, or the environment at home and around the globe. As American foundations turn their attention to problems that span borders and that are shaped by globalization processes, having some clarity about the core rationale that guides giving will be critical. Many of the frameworks and tools that have been helpful to grantmakers in the USA have direct application when the frame of giving shifts to the international stage.

The dearth of analyses of the role of American philanthropy abroad does not necessarily mean that material for such studies is lacking; on the contrary, it suggests the existence of fertile ground for investigation which should be of interest to international educators and scholars. The audience for this research includes international organizations, governmental agencies, and NGOs involved in international assistance, international development, and higher education and secondary education development which seek to understand what private foundations do, why they decide to do what they do, and how they deliver their mission and vision.

In addition, this book is for foundation boards, presidents, program directors, and officers, particularly if they are involved in or seek more information about building the educational capital of developing countries. And finally, this book is for those who are looking for an insider's view on the world of foundations, philanthropists, and international developers.

New York, NY, USA   Fabrice Jaumont
www.fabricejaumont.net

ACKNOWLEDGMENTS

Without the support and encouragement of many individuals and organizations, this book would not have been completed. For their assistance and encouragement at various stages, special appreciation is expressed to:

Richard Arum, who gave unselfishly of his time, knowledge, and efforts in directing this study, guiding my theoretical inquiries in its early stages and keeping a watchful eye over my academic explorations. Teboho Moja, who brought wisdom and expertise on African higher education and US foundations in Africa; Laetitia Atlani-Duault, who helped with orchestrating the myriad voices that shaped this book; and Dana Burde and Philip Hosay, who offered suggestions and encouragement from the very beginning of this project many years ago all the way to the final stages. I would like to thank other individuals who positively influenced me during my doctoral studies or contributed to my research: Jonathan Zimmerman; Cynthia Miller-Idriss; Ian McLeod; Olivier Bouin; Alessandra Benedicty; N'Dri Assie-Lumuba; Thomas Asher; Alessia Lefebure; Marshall Thomas; Zehra Hashmi; Alissa Rae Funderburk; Tieisha Tift; Edith Bon; Bruce and Darcey Hale; Jane Ross; and a particular thank you to Charlotte Collett; Jonathan Collett,, Jack Klempay, and Maggie Liston.

A special thank you to the editors of Palgrave Macmillan who have believed in the book from day one. Appreciation is also expressed to those who opened their archives and records and gave of their time in granting interviews, in making information for this study available. Appreciation is expressed in particular to Sue Grant-Lewis; John Butler-Adams; Jonathan Friedman; Andrea Johnson; Stuart Saunders; Raul Davion; Joyce Moock; Kole Shettima; Tamara Fox; Phillip Griffith; Claudia Fritelli; Dina El'Khawaga; Patricia Rosenfield; Neil Grabois; Janice Petrovich; Narciso Matos; Tade Akin Aina; William Moses; Gara LaMarche; David Court; and a particular thank you to Vartan Gregorian who accepted to write the foreword to this book and whom I admire immensely.

Particular acknowledgment for Megan Lindow who granted me permission to use her personal archives which included over 100 interview transcripts of scholars, university administrators, and students in Africa.

Finally, I dedicate this book to my wife, Nathalie, and daughters, Cléa and Félicie, who brought me the extra strengths to complete this project, and to my parents, Martine and Serge, who have always believed in me.

CONTENTS

List of Figures

LIST OF TABLES

CHAPTER 1

Introduction: American Philanthropy and the Rebirth of Higher Education in Africa

Philanthropic foundations have been active participants in the development of higher education since the end of the nineteenth century. They played a formative role in the creation of modern colleges and universities—a mission that extends beyond US borders in a global effort to develop human capital. Originating from private fortunes, independently managed and subject to few legal restrictions, private foundations are enterprising entities that sit between the public and the private spheres. Their role in society is accepted in part because they are expected to serve the public good and advance a variety of social objectives. Today, philanthropic foundations are builders of "knowledge societies," defined by United Nations Educational, Scientific, and Cultural Organization (UNESCO) as entities that foster knowledge sharing. For these foundations, the diffusion of information and communication technologies creates new opportunities for economic development. Taking into account the climate of criticism that currently surrounds the manner in which development priorities are set by various governmental and international agencies, US foundations have positioned themselves strategically in the sector by providing innovative solutions, spearheading new possibilities in development work, and promoting the sharing of knowledge and information in developing societies. In doing so, they mitigate the criticism leveled at international aid providers while defining and setting development priorities. This special positioning is not accidental, as foundations pay close attention to their respective roles and the legitimacy of their work. Foundations' influence is particularly noticeable in areas such as health, human rights, agriculture, and international development. However, it is clear that foundations are particularly active in higher education, as this sector represents a niche largely ignored by governments, international organizations, and development agencies in many parts of the world.

While almost 100 foundations invested in the development of higher education in Africa between 2003 and 2013, this book focuses on seven foundations: the Carnegie Corporation of New York, Ford Foundation, John D. and

© The Editor(s) (if applicable) and The Author(s) 2016
F. Jaumont, *Unequal Partners*, Philanthropy and Education,
DOI 10.1057/978-1-137-59348-1_1

Catherine T. MacArthur Foundation, The Rockefeller Foundation, The William and Flora Hewlett Foundation, The Andrew W. Mellon Foundation, and The Kresge Foundation.[1] Together, these foundations make up the Partnership for Higher Education in Africa (PHEA) that invested close to $500 million in the development of African higher education between 2000 and 2010. This research includes a survey of 12,000 grants made to academic institutions, research networks, and other organizations involved in Africa's development between 2000 and 2013, as well as interviews of grantees representing universities and research centers located in nine countries in Africa, including South Africa, Nigeria, Ghana, Kenya, Mozambique, Tanzania, Uganda, Egypt, and Madagascar. To put these foundations' work in perspective, Chapters 2 and 3 explore at length the ecology of US foundations and higher education in Africa.

With more US foundations turning their attention to global issues, partnerships and strategic collaborations between private funders have gained ground. However, partnerships between foundations are not always guaranteed to produce effective results. In a famous essay on collaboration, Paul Brest, former president of the Hewlett Foundation, suggested that foundations could work together to generate better ideas and build broader constituencies while increasing the amount of money available to address common goals. However, he also warned against the relative drawbacks that collaborations may generate:

> Collaboration has inevitable up-front costs in the time and effort spent in communicating and making decisions together with one's partners. The process can often be frustrating, and a beneficial outcome is hardly assured. At the end of the day, the extra effort is justified only if it has greater impact in improving people's lives.[2]

Numerous factors at the foundations' institutional, intra-organizational, and environmental levels can explain these drawbacks. Strategic partnerships require an understanding of these factors to avoid derailment or damage to the foundations' reputation. Chapters 4, 5, and 6 address these issues and explore the commonalities of philanthropic foundations. Collaboration can also be complicated by the unequal relationships between foundations and their grantees. These relationships form intricate mechanisms through which foundations leverage funds and maximize impact. Chapters 7, 8, and 9 focus on these specific matters by closely examining the question of legitimacy related to US foundations.

The ensuing empirical chapters examine the multiple relationships that informed US foundations' engagement with higher education institutions in Africa: the relationship on-the-ground between foundations and universities, the rapport among various foundations in Africa and in the USA, and the relationship between foundations and their dynamics of legitimation. As such these chapters gauge the types of interactions that determine collaboration and generate impact in a wide and complex field that is higher education on the African continent. The chapters trace the contours of educational philanthropy and identify various institutional factors that shape higher education development. In order to positively impact higher education in Africa, US foundations constantly revisit their approaches and pay particular attention to their beneficiaries. Sources of motivation and organizational mechanisms are analyzed to demonstrate that foundations engaged in partnerships use collaboration as a strategy to generate and maximize their impact, which, in turn, help them justify their choices, worldviews, practices, or what Hammack and Heydemann (2009) call their "philanthropic projection of institutional logic abroad." Foundations negotiate between mutual support and their common cause to generate added value through partnerships without sacrificing their independence and mission.

This study is based on data extracted from summaries of the PHEA's meeting minutes, email correspondences, notes, evaluation drafts, reports, and publications. These documents depict the numerous interactions between partnering foundations, and between grantors and grantees, focusing on a set of interrelated and overlapping efforts by seven foundations. The data set is supplemented with an array of interviews, drawing attention to the question of how foundations both establish and make use of their legitimacy, authority, and capability to effect change in the world. Interviewees included seven program officers, six directors, four advisors and associates, and three vice-presidents and presidents. These individuals were the main actors involved in the PHEA. Qualitative data were based on actors' retrospective accounts of partnership activity. Subjects had previous or current affiliation or involvement with the selected institutions, including those who dealt with grant application and requirements within said institutions. These individuals were interviewed in their official capacities (whether past or present) revealing the depth of engagement that characterized the PHEA. Additionally, over 100 interviews of individuals in Africa were included in the research. The transcripts served as a basis for various foundation-led publication projects. The interviews were conducted in 2010 and included both identified and unidentified interviewees at several African institutions. The interviews included grantees' broad reflections on higher education in their respective countries. Each subject was asked to comment on aspects of higher education that might have changed as a result of the relationships and processes that took place between their institution and the foundations. The respondents included students, professors, researchers, and research assistants, grant administrators, and university administrators in various universities in several countries, such as the University of Jos, University of Ibadan and Obafemi Awolowo University in Nigeria, the University of Cape Town and the University of the Witwatersrand in South Africa, University of Dar es Salaam in Tanzania, Makerere University in Uganda, and the University of Cairo in Egypt, among several others. The sample also includes a few administrators from academic and research networks.

This research represents a nuanced analysis of a US-led foundation initiative of uncommon ambition, comprising seven foundations with a shared commitment to strengthen capacity in higher education in Sub-Saharan African universities. From a sociological perspective, this work contextualizes new philanthropic trends and examines the conditions under which philanthropy can be effective, the impasses that foundations often face, and the novel context in which philanthropy operates today. This topic engages two issues around which there is emerging interest among researchers and practitioners alike: The shifting grounds on which higher education is positioned globally and the role of global philanthropy within these changing contexts. These issues are especially important currently in a moment when higher education is once again recognized as a driver of development and economic growth, knowledge economies dependent on a highly educated population are displacing economies predicated on manufacturing and unskilled labor, and higher education is coming under pressure to adapt to new conditions. Foundations play an important role in facilitating this transformation and in responding to these new conditions, albeit in ways that are not well understood or widely accepted.

Moreover, many of the more recent publications on foundations have been tacked between two extremes: at once excessively broad and generic in subject matter in their efforts and analysis or excessively focused on one single philanthropic organization. This depiction of US foundations looks at conditions under which philanthropic efforts were successful in achieving their intent to act in concert. This study examines the constraints and conditions that allow foundations to effect change and influence grantees, governments, and other foundations alike. Exploring these areas of inquiry offers a nuanced theory of how institutions can influence external actors and initiate transformation. While the focus is the PHEA, the discussion is generalized to all US foundations that have invested in or established a relationship with an African higher education institution. With millions of dollars invested in universities and academic networks across the continent, the Partnership is at the forefront of higher education development in Africa. However, many other non-Partnership foundations were heavily engaged in the field during this period such as The Atlantic Philanthropies, Bill & Melinda Gates Foundation, W. K. Kellogg Foundation,The McKnight Foundation, The Michael and Susan Dell Foundation, Charles Stewart Mott Foundation, and The David and Lucile Packard Foundation to name but a few. Furthermore, broader issues such as institutional transformation, capacity building, and the development of the higher education sector will be addressed as well as the role of outside funders and developers in higher education reforms on the African continent.

Although higher education is being developed in several African countries, a majority of universities on the continent are still plagued by unstable national political contexts that constrain academic freedom and limit potential support from more external donors. Higher education in Africa in the early 2000s was characterized by a small number of universities per country and low enrollment ratios at all levels. The whole sector was hampered by multiple weaknesses, as Akilagpa Sawyerr, former Secretary-General of the Association of African Universities, wrote:

> In most African countries, conditions for research have been severely compromised as manifest by the generally poor remuneration, heavy teaching loads, inability to mentor young faculty, and inadequate infrastructure.[3]

The sector was plagued by challenges such as aging faculty members and a lack of incentives to attract younger staff. The issue of a continued brain drain tendency, that afflicts most African countries, was pervasive. Moreover, scholars such as Benneh et al. (2004) argue that inadequate financial and logistical support from national governments, weak private sector backing, and few private contributions to universities can all be considered insurmountable obstacles to any form of institutional development. Furthermore, recent literature on African higher education confirms that African scholars are calling for more involvement in the inception and implementation of programs (Tiyambe Zeleza and Olukoshi 2004; Afolayan 2007; Moja 2007). In several instances, the question of program ownership is emphasized as an underrated and understudied dimension of the institutional relationship between donors and beneficiaries, particularly within the context of international development. The desire to maintain ownership of a project, concept, or institution can be a manifestation of a beneficiary's resistance to an undesired transformation, calling into question the legitimacy of the donor's intentions. Moreover, this resistance to change also reflects universities' inability to generate an endogenous model of development as opposed to an inherited one. African scholars still ask how universities can transcend the mechanism by which Western institutions are inherited so that universities may serve as an engine for African development, instead of falling victim to Westernization.

Critics of philanthropy point to the arrogance of funders, their poor planning, unresponsiveness, lack of ethical conduct, and compromised work. As these issues are raised locally in the USA with reference to school reforms, similar issues could easily be raised with regard to US foundations' funding of education initiatives outside of the USA. Nevertheless, these foundations' accomplishments are particularly remarkable in light of the relatively small sums of monies that are involved, as well as their ability to leverage funds from outside sources. US foundations have demonstrated a certain know-how in maximizing their investments, impact, and influence, particularly on institutions of higher learning. By expanding their scope and expertise to higher education in Africa, foundations asserted their role in the construction of knowledge societies on a global scale—providing support to academic institutions, research centers, and scholastic networks. They also extended their own views of knowledge production to the rest of the world through their programs activities. The need for further empirical explorations and comparative examinations of foundation-led social change abroad is clear. This discussion provides a perspective on private foundations and the complexity of philanthropic action. It explores the question of legitimacy with an institutional lens, and offers a bird's eye view on foundation grantmaking over a specific region and time frame. This research offers an analysis of US philanthropies and higher education development, and explores the relationship between foundations and their grantees in Africa.

In recent years, philanthropic foundations of international renown have advocated for the importance of higher education in the economic development of Africa. This shift in objectives represents a strategic repositioning in the ecology of international developers, as the concept of "knowledge societies"—

whereby the effective creation, use, and dissemination of knowledge is increasingly the key to sustainable economic and social development—continues to gain traction. Researchers have identified a certain amount of liberty granted to foundations in comparison to other international organizations or government agencies. Indeed, foundations have several advantages that other bodies do not have: they are independent; they are not under pressure for short-term results; they can take risks; and they have developed a heightened sensitivity to specific problems. It is with this knowledge that this book poses the question: Is it possible for foundations to generate value in the field of higher education in Africa and help transform universities while improving their condition? The relationships between US grantmaking institutions and their grantees are, by nature, unequal—the great dilemma of philanthropy. However, universities are becoming increasingly important players in the global market. Strong educational institutions can be valuable for a country wishing to project itself and its leaders onto the world stage, even if those institutions are modeled on Western paradigms. US foundations may well provide benefits to the countries that receive their support; indeed, the existence of international foundations all around the world is based on this very premise.

NOTES

1. See Table 13 in the appendix for a complete list.
2. Brest (2006), p. 1.
3. Sawyerr (2004), p. 211.

BIBLIOGRAPHY

Afolayan, Michael O. 2007. *Higher education in postcolonial Africa: Paradigms of development, decline, and dilemmas.* Trenton: Africa World Press.

Benneh, George, Mariama Awumbila, and Paul Effah. 2004. *African universities, the private sector and civil society, forging partnerships for development.* Accra: African Regional Council of the International Association of University Presidents.

Brest, Paul. 2006. *On collaboration (or how many foundations does it take to change a light bulb?).* Menlo Park: Hewlett Foundation.

——— (eds.). 2006. *Transformation in higher education—Global pressures and local realities,* Higher Education Dynamics, vol. 10. Dordrecht: Springer.

Hammack, David C., and Steven Heydemann (eds.). 2009. *Globalization, philanthropy, and civil society. Projecting institutional logics abroad.* Bloomington: Indiana University Press.

Moja Teboho and Cloete Nico:Transformation Tensions in Higher Education: Equity, Efficiency, and Development. *Social Research—An International Quartely of the Social Science.* Vol. 72, No. 3, Fall 2005, pp. 693–722. The New School.

Sawyerr, Akilagpa. 2004. African universities and the challenge of research capacity development. *JHEA/RESA* 2(1): 211–240.

Zeleza, Paul Tiyambe, and Adebayo Olukoshi. 2004. *African universities in the twenty-first century,* vol. 2. Dakar: Council for the Development of Social Science Research in Africa.

PART I

The Ecology of U.S. Foundations in Africa

CHAPTER 2

Century-Old Philanthropic Interests in Africa's Higher Education

Foundations' considerable influence, accumulated over decades of strategic grantmaking in the field of US higher education, remains unrivaled and remarkable considering the relatively small size of their investments to academic institutions. As such, foundations play an important part in the reshaping of higher education in the USA and in many parts of the world. This privileged status has been thoroughly examined in relevant literature. Hollis (1938), for instance, described the role of Carnegie Corporation of New York and The Rockefeller Foundation in the early part of the twentieth century, illustrating their lasting influence in the development of colleges in the USA. These foundations shaped institutions directly, by providing grants that supported the addition of new facilities and the production of knowledge, and indirectly, by pressuring universities to adapt to the changing realities of the field. Curti and Nash (1965) further discuss the phenomenon of indirect influence, asserting that foundations raised the standards of higher education in the USA by concentrating on a select number of institutions. This forced others to reform in a "survival of the fittest" race that they saw as "thoroughly compatible with the social ideas of the industrialists-philanthropists responsible for the foundations."[1]

The current situation of foundation patronage in higher education has changed drastically; the main grantmakers in the field share a set of objectives that is very different from those who invested in colleges and universities in the early twentieth century. However, foundations have continued to strategically concentrate their support on a favored group of institutions. In their study of foundation grants in 2001, Frumkin & Kaplan (in Hammack and Anheier 2010) indicate that almost "twenty-five hundred organizations involved in higher education received a foundation grant in 2001, but twenty-five of them—1 percent— accounted for almost 30 percent of the money."[2] This group includes the most respected private research universities in the USA: Harvard University, Princeton University, Stanford University, Yale University, Columbia University, University of Pennsylvania, Duke University,

© The Editor(s) (if applicable) and The Author(s) 2016
F. Jaumont, *Unequal Partners*, Philanthropy and Education,
DOI 10.1057/978-1-137-59348-1_2

Johns Hopkins University, and New York University, among equally prestigious public institutions. This targeted selection approach is central to the strategies of development-oriented philanthropic foundations in African higher education, as the following chapters demonstrate. Do foundations select these institutions to minimize the risk of their investment? Do they simply introduce competition for scarce resources which these top institutions continuously manage to grab, even as others try to emulate them? Are these universities successful precisely because they comply to the foundations' objectives? This system of favoritism creates a divide between elite institutions and others—arguably affecting the quality and delivery of knowledge throughout the higher education system by putting pressure on less endowed institutions, overwhelming professors, and impacting college affordability.

Much to their credit, foundations have been highly influential in the development of student financial aid, libraries, and adult education. They have helped create educational opportunity for minorities, fashioned new standards for courses and credits, encouraged the development of new disciplines, and advocated for improvements in faculty compensation. On this particular aspect, Cheit and Lobman (1979) note that foundations help academics "escape from subservience to patronage." Until the first foundation grants of the late 1910s and early 1920s, only independently wealthy faculty members could pursue research. Foundation support for faculty members leveled the playing field and revealed foundations' powerful influence on academic disciplines. These authors conclude that the foundations' funding and vision had a profound impact on the structure of higher education in transforming and modernizing educational systems: "Foundations have helped—and more often led—the colleges from a somewhat disorganized collection of institutions into a modern, diverse system of higher education that is admired throughout the world."[3] The foundations' leadership role arose over decades of strategic grantmaking to higher education—when academic institutions were still in their infancy and the role of government in higher education was almost non-existent. Without competition from financial contributors or governmental constraints, foundations effectively asserted their leadership in the field of higher education. For instance, by supplementing grants with conditions such as higher admission requirements or a retirement system for professors, the early foundations succeeded not only in shaping higher education in the USA but also in reinforcing and legitimizing their role as developers of knowledge-producing institutions.

Early education-oriented foundations such as Carnegie Corporation of New York, the Rockefeller Foundation, and The Phelps Stokes Fund, among others, played a significant role in restructuring public education in the USA; much of the institutional and structural framework they helped consolidate remains in place today. The Carnegie Foundation for the Advancement of Teaching allocated funding exclusively to higher education that resulted in a change in college admissions requirements, which, in turn, modified and standardized high school curricula throughout the country (Condliffe Lagemann 1983). The Rockefeller Foundation expanded state responsibility for public education in the South by using evidence-based social research to influence education policy. Thus, private funds were used to leverage public funding and influence the development and structuring of secondary and higher education nationwide. However, these foundations' influence over education provoked harsh criticism, illustrated by vehement opponents such as Horace Coon (1938) who coined the infamous slogan "When the State steps in, the foundation steps out."[4] This reflected both the spirit of the time and foundations' tendency to pull back from their engagement when public funds were successfully leveraged. Nevertheless, grants may also have the opposite effect by disrupting practices and equilibriums in the systems targeted for change, as many scholars have noted throughout the years (Hollis 1938; Wormser 1958; Curti 1963; Cheit and Lobman 1979 O'Connell 1987; Nielsen 1996; Dowie 2002). These authors, whose criticisms are discussed at length in the following chapters, question the adequacy of foundation-supported solutions in the US context. The following section continues this discussion within the context of African higher education.

HIGHER EDUCATION IN AFRICA AND THE PRESENCE OF US FOUNDATIONS

Contrary to popular belief, higher education has a very long and distinguished history in Africa—dating well before Western-style universities were established on the continent in the nineteenth century. From the third century BC, which saw the creation of the Alexandria Museum and Library, to Christian monasteries that spanned multiple countries, the African continent has been home to renowned centers of scholarship and higher learning. Many of these institutions were influenced by religion, and Africa lays claim to the world's oldest Islamic universities and some of the world's oldest surviving universities: Ez-Zitouna madrassa founded in Tunis in 731; al Qairawiyyin mosque university in Fez in 859; Al-Azhar mosque university in 969 in Cairo; and the famous Sankore mosque university in Timbuktu which was built in the twelfth century by Mansa Kankan Musa (1280–1337), the "King of Kings" of the wealthy Malian Empire. Documented as the richest person to have ever lived, his fortune was worth the equivalent of $400 billion in today's currency, with which he built numerous educational center and mosques across Africa. These centers of higher learning influenced the world.

The West's debt to Islamic and Arab science is well-established and acknowledged. As African scholars often remind us, the modern university that was brought to Africa by the colonial powers is as much Western in origin as it is Islamic. For instance, Y. G-M Lulat (2005) writes:

> The Europeans acquired from the Muslims … a huge corpus of knowledge… Second, they learned rationalism combined with…the secular investigative approach typical of Arab natural science… a sophisticated disciplinary map of knowledge… a host of academic subjects.[5]

The Islamic origin of what we now know as Western-style universities was introduced to Europe through Spain (and by extension North Africa). Thus, Western models of higher education were influenced by North-African and Middle-Eastern knowledge-producing institutions—a view which is echoed by other African scholars (Mamdani and Diouf 1994; Ajavi et al. 1996; Assie-Lumumba 2006; Afolayan 2007; Mamdani 2012). Two opposing axes of higher education development in Africa occurred during the colonial era: on one hand, missionary work (religious and vocational education) and on the other, Western-style universities in settler colonies. Scholars have observed that vocational education increased in the second half of the nineteenth century in several parts of central and southern Africa in part due to Christian American women who formed their own foreign missionary societies (Curti 1963). A myriad of other religious proselytizers developed vocational schools for boys and girls, training the local peoples in agriculture and industry. Finally, missionaries also founded modern Western-style colleges and universities in Africa in the early nineteenth century. These institutions were largely concentrated in European settler colonies such as South Africa, Algeria, Sierra Leone, and Liberia's newly established territories of African diaspora resettlement.

US foundations have been involved extensively with African universities and higher education networks, some for almost a century. The Rockefeller Foundation's international activities started in the early 1910s and positioned the foundation as an indisputable pioneer of technical assistance and a proponent of institution building and university development throughout its history (Coleman and Court 1993). The International Health Board of the Rockefeller Foundation, established in 1913 to extend the public health work of the Rockefeller Sanitary Commission for the Eradication of Hookworm Disease worldwide, was the first of the Rockefeller philanthropic boards to have extensive contacts in Africa. In the 1920s, Rockefeller philanthropies began to fund initiatives that focused on African educators. For instance, the Rockefeller Foundation, through the International Education Board (IEB), contributed $6000 toward the Fund's Educational Commission to East Africa and co-sponsored a tour of African-American colleges and universities in the South for a group of African educators (Gray 1941). Following this initiative, several Africans received fellowships to study in American universities. Through inter-board discussions on education and health in Africa with the Board of the Phelps-Stokes Fund, the leaders of the IEB and other Rockefeller philanthropies began to consider how US philanthropy could support vocational training and the medical field in Africa.

In *The Best Fields for Philanthropy*, Andrew Carnegie, once considered the richest man in the world, wrote, "the best uses to which a millionaire can devote [his] surplus is first the founding of a university."[6] It is no surprise that the Carnegie Corporation of New York has become a champion for higher education around the world. Under Frederick Keppel, Carnegie Corporation of New York expended resources in regions of the British Empire, including the Union of South Africa and other British colonies between 1923 and 1941.

During the summer of 1927, Keppel and James Bertram (a trustee as well as the foundation's secretary) visited Africa for two months—a trip that had great influence over the foundation's commitment to education in Africa. As such, both men were early pioneers in the endeavor of educational philanthropy in Africa. Similarly, they had to think about the role and place of their foundation among international funders and agencies, and the consequences of their funding choices. In a December 1927 report to the Board, Keppel and Bertram expressed a series of both negative and positive considerations for Carnegie Corporation of New York to adhere to when entering the field of African education. The Corporation should:

> Avoid relieving either public or private agencies from their own duty. Avoid taking steps which would involve the Corporation in current political controversies, especially in Kenya and South Africa, where political questions arouse the strongest feelings. Avoid entering fields which could better be dealt with by other non-African agencies [they meant The Rockefeller Foundation and public health work among the natives]. Avoid embarking upon a program involving a group of specific grants in any field before a foundation has been laid in informed public opinion and representative group organizations.[7]

This prescient excerpt expresses both the potential risks of mindless philanthropy and a strategy to avoid these risks. It also shows how Carnegie Corporation of New York savvy foundation officers gauged the presence of other players in the field before unfolding their own strategy for Africa. More importantly, it underlines the role of multiple social agents, which had the potential to maximize or denigrate the foundation's legitimacy in the field. These included local public and private agencies, local representative group organizations, governmental and political bodies, non-African agencies and public opinion. Additionally, it demonstrates how Corporation's board functioned as an ultimate legitimation agent by approving and enforcing the program officers' recommendations, therefore legitimizing the foundation's course of action, staff time, and investment in a wide variety of operations.

During the years of colonization, higher education development in Africa progressed at slow pace until the end of World War II. African governments were largely distrustful of modern educated Africans and their demands for independence and emancipation from colonial rule. Higher education was also a contentious issue in countries which managed to gain their independence, as the few existing universities were elitist and patterned on European models. There was a need to make higher education more relevant to Africa's developmental needs and post-independence sociocultural context, and more accessible to students of different socio-economic backgrounds. At that time, universities attempted to bolster national prestige, train a highly skilled labor force, and create a national elite (Zeleza 2006). In the 1960s and 1970s, universities expanded disciplinary and curricula offerings from the arts and social sciences to include professional fields of study and graduate programs. During those years, foundations were heavily involved with African higher education. Carnegie Corporation of New York conducted a university development program that spanned until the mid-1970s and established a variety of grants to African universities. The Rockefeller Foundation was also very involved with steady contributions and a commitment to university development.

The following two decades focused almost exclusively on basic education, as higher education was perceived as a luxury that African nations could not afford. The field of African higher education was simply ignored by all foreign donors; most US foundations had left the field by the early 1980s. The field of higher education in Africa witnessed a dramatic shift, as Coleman and Court (1993) noted, a "pendulum swung away from universities to rural development, informal and vocational education, and the poorest of the poor as top priorities."[8] Yet, in the 1980s and 1990s, universities gradually became to be seen as engines of development and were expected to provide leadership through the production of knowledge, the development of human resources, and the provision of service to the communities. Responding to changes, US foundations provided funding for a number of projects. The philosophy of the time assumed that the rate of return on investments in primary education was higher than that of investments in higher education. Therefore, developing countries were discouraged from diverting their scarce resources toward higher education. This belief was championed by the World Bank and the International Monetary Fund, among others. However, the end of the 1990s experienced a shift away from this policy toward a new understanding of the impact of higher education on the development of primary education and other areas. Thus, a holistic approach to education was promoted as a prerequisite to creating change in specific areas of human development. In the words of Samoff and Carroll (2004), higher education in Africa went "from favored focus to disparaged wastrel to development engine in two decades."[9] At the turn of the new millennium, higher education in Africa was characterized by a small number of universities per country and low enrollment ratios at all levels. The sector was plagued by challenges such as an aging faculty and a lack of incentives to attract younger staff, not to mention the continued brain drain which saw countries in Sub-Saharan African lose a tremendous amount of their educated and skilled population as a result of emigration to more developed countries. Despite the renewed focus on higher education, these issues proved to be difficult challenges for development agencies to overcome. Additionally, insufficient monetary and logistical backing from African governments, along with insignificant private sector support to universities, were all insoluble hindrances to any form of institutional development. To some extent, the limited resources of universities make them vulnerable, dependent, and susceptible to the influence of various stakeholders. Although there can be a positive exchange between donors and beneficiaries, their relationships are nonetheless unequal, as Coleman and Court (1993) note:

Within limits imposed by political circumstance and university support donors can assist in creating a favorable environment for academic freedom. By the same token they can help to weaken or constrain it. In some measure this negative contribution is inevitable not simply because the institutionalization of academic freedom has to be an internal process, to which external donors can make a limited contribution, but also because of the inherently unequal nature of the relationship between donor and recipient.[10]

In this passage, the asymmetrical relationship between grantors and grantees is described as an inevitable obstacle to institutional change, one that can potentially limit the role and impact of grantors. Considering the influence of grantmakers over funding priorities and the agenda of higher education, the recurring theme of inequality between grantors and their beneficiaries will be closely examined in this book.

During the 1990s, US foundations targeted development in Africa and viewed universities as engines of development, providing the bulk of their funding to higher education institutions that offered assistance to communities and governments. At the time, universities provided services through policy research and the implementation of projects within communities. The foundations' support to the field of higher education in Africa was noteworthy as it empowered universities that played a critical role in responding to bigger needs brought about by political upheavals and a new economic order. African societies of the 1990s faced many challenges that required new cooperative ways of thinking from existing donors, in order to tackle issues too large for one funder alone. Governments and universities were undergoing transformation almost concurrently—a situation that triggered additional competition for scarcer financial resources, as universities navigated around harsh budget cuts that forced them to eliminate crucial programs and services to the community they served. The involvement of foundations presented universities with fresh funding in critical areas, such as research, for knowledge development. Foundations also focused on providing technical training, which helped provide people on the ground with better skills to respond to the various crises. The field of higher education was gradually becoming fertile—filled with promises for international developers and agencies operating in the sector.

At the dawn of the millennium, universities were criticized for not being responsive enough to the needs of the external environment within which they operated. This debate about the transformation of higher education was not new as it already surfaced in the early 1970s when the relevance and value of African universities were questioned. During the 1990s, higher education transformation underscored the importance of knowledge for social and economic development. The debated issue of relevance called into question the universities' responsiveness to contemporary socio-economic issues.

To understand this impact on institutions, one must examine the different functions of universities and the capacity of the institutions (of both the faculty and management) to deliver or carry out their functions. Knowledge development and dissemination, curriculum transformation and teaching innovation, community service and development, and access and equity were among the key areas of focus targeted by foundations. Research grants to universities served two main purposes. The first purpose was the development of a knowledge base to address social issues and to develop materials for teaching purposes. The second purpose was the development of capacity within the institution to conduct research by strengthening the existing capacity and training students, who were then subsequently attracted to academic careers.

The need for curriculum transformation became urgent as universities responded to new needs. Curriculum transformation entailed a re-evaluation of knowledge-producing strategies within the developing context. Grants were made to departments within universities to conduct seminars aimed at reviewing the accuracy of curriculum content in subjects like history, allowing for changes to respond to new needs in areas such as economics and law. The history department of the University of Zimbabwe received funding from Ford Foundation to host a seminar aimed at reviewing the history and impact of Zimbabwe's struggle for independence. The researchers' main objectives were to document the past and contribute to reform processes. Elsewhere on the continent, universities promoted debates on the identification of relevant knowledge and its integration into various curricula. For instance, a project implemented by the Center for Higher Education Transformation (CHET) in South Africa examined issues regarding curriculum reform. CHET, a non-teaching agency in higher education, was well positioned to take a broader look at curriculum issues compared with education schools. The CHET study concluded that curriculum transformation entailed a careful understanding of the learner as well as the way that knowledge was produced, organized, and distributed (Cloete et al. 1997).

Foundations funded projects that addressed urgent issues in communities within which universities were located, enabling them to play their role in providing services to their own communities. Issues such as deforestation, civil rights, poverty reduction, conflict resolution and peace, and economic revitalization were covered by foundations. The problem of limited access to universities has always been a continent-wide problem. Students have failed to gain access to higher education due to shortages of spots available in universities. In other cases, denial of access has been due to poor school conditions that leave students inadequately prepared for college. Contrary to the situation in many African countries, limited access to higher education in countries like Namibia and South Africa has been based on race due to apartheid era policies that promoted inequities in the system of education. Ford Foundation supported programs that expanded educational and training opportunities for Blacks in higher education. Grants were made to universities for the development and improvement of alternative routes. The South African projects funded by the foundation had as their objective the preparation of Black students for university entry. The University of KwaZulu-Natal developed a program referred to as the "Teach-Test-Teach" that served as an alternative selection technique for Black students seeking university admission. A number of institutions in South Africa also initiated student internship programs funded by the foundation. The programs matched Black graduate student interns with senior faculty as mentors for joint research, publications, and work experience. The goal was to recruit Black students for graduate programs, with the specific intention of attracting them to future academic careers. An unintended outcome was that local communities became more accessible to the universities, due to the involvement of junior researchers who spoke the languages spoken by the communities served by those universities. The communities also benefited from this relationship by accessing previously inaccessible university resources.

CAPACITY BUILDING AND INSTITUTIONAL DEVELOPMENT

"Capacity building," a concept which originated in the 1960s, increasingly draws the attention of funders, international developers, non-governmental organizations, universities, and other public-interest organizations. Capacity building varies among donors, as their approach depends on their values and organizational structure (Whyte 2004). Some funders have referred to capacity building as a renewed focus on institutional outputs. Others have put more emphasis on research outputs and the impact of research products on the university's immediate environment. In the case of Africa's higher education sector, institution building was historically a priority, especially in the period after independence was attained by many African states. This was necessitated by the departure of expatriates who occupied most of the positions in higher education. Institutions like the University of Ife and the University of Ibadan benefited from Ford Foundation's initiatives for capacity development in the 1970s and 1980s. Unfortunately, universities in Africa today continue to be criticized for the shortage of qualified faculty and the impact it has on the quality of education they offer.

In the 1990s, capacity development involved a reassessment of technical cooperation with a renewed interest in focusing on faculty development issues as institutions prepared themselves for the devastating impact of HIV/AIDS on faculty and students, and ultimately on the environment within which higher education is located. Grants were made to universities to conduct research on the development of a new generation of academics. There was a new focus on academic networks accompanied by a departure from capacity building understood as a method for structural adjustment and policy reform. The Millennium Development Goals were the key drivers for donors, who showed a greater awareness to participatory approaches and recognized the importance of local ownership in successful grantmaking. As a result, universities became more aware of the need to play an active role in the development of their faculty and the cultivation of young scholars for retention as future faculty. Universities in Africa in the 1990s responded to the increasing importance of knowledge for social and economic development. Knowledge production became a major issue, as the need to develop learning-centered nations put more pressure on the higher education sector to provide leadership in knowledge production, interpretation, and consumption.

At the beginning of the twenty-first century, there was a possibility that Africa could be left behind in the reorganization of the world around new knowledge networks with the spread of information and communication technology (ICT). The knowledge gap between Africa and the Western world was widening. African universities' contributions were becoming insignificant in the production as well as use of knowledge produced mainly at the time by industrialized countries. The transformation of higher education systems on the African continent was more than necessary, and several US foundations felt they had a role to play in this historical project. Although several African universities had begun to transform at the turn of the millennium, many universities continued to be plagued by power struggles within their home countries. This instability, along with the complexity of these institutions' socio-political heritage, ultimately constrained academic freedom and limited the potential for support from external donors. Furthermore, several prominent voices in African higher education call for greater ownership in the development and financing of programs and institutions by foreign donors. As John Ssebuwufu, Director of Research Programs at the Association of African Universities in Ghana, writes, "The African institution must fully own the programs, and not be left feeling that the programs are an imposition with minimum input from their side."[11] Foreign and private donors were becoming increasingly sensitive to this point of view, as James Coleman and David Court's 1993 analysis on university development in the third world confirms:

> Because academic freedom in a given context has to be embedded in the institutions and forms of that society, an external agency can contribute only partially to the process of institutionalization which builds academic freedom. Being inextricably linked with the development of a sense of national identity, institutionalization of anything is a process in which there are obvious inherent psychological limitations to external assistance. By its very nature, an institution is something a people must feel is their own, an integral and distinctive part of the fabric of their society.[12]

Program ownership is an underrated and understudied aspect of the institutional interaction between donor and beneficiary, particularly in the field of international development. The desire to own a project, concept, or institution reveals a resistance to undesirable transformations, and calls into question the legitimacy of a donor's intentions. Moreover, this resistance to external influence highlights universities' inability to generate their own endogenous model out of an inherited one. Echoing Eric Ashby's 1964 reflection on the mechanism for the inheritance of the Western institutions, contemporary African scholars still ask how their universities are to be made African such that they serve as an engine for African development, not Westernization (Cloete et al. 2006).

NOTES

1. Curti and Nash (1965), p. 262.
2. Frumkin & Kaplan (in Hammack and Anheier 2010), p. 105.
3. Cheit and Lobman (1979), p. 2.
4. Coon (1938), p. 55.
5. Lulat (2005), p. 16.
6. Carnegie (1889), p. 18.
7. Keppel and Bertram (1927), p. 9.
8. Coleman and Court (1993), p. 16.
9. Samoff and Carroll (2004), p. 201.
10. Coleman and Court (1993), p. 332.
11. Fisher Karin & Lindow Megan. Africa Attracts Renewed Attention from American Universities in The Chronicle of Higher Education, July 18, 2008.
12. Coleman and Court (1993), p. 331.

BIBLIOGRAPHY

Afolayan, Michael O. 2007. *Higher education in postcolonial Africa: Paradigms of development, decline, and dilemmas.* Trenton: Africa World Press.

Ajayi, Ade J.F., K.H. Goma Lameck, and Ampah G. Johnson. 1996. *The African experience with higher education.* Accra: The Association of African Universities.

Ashby, Eric. 1964. *African universities and Western tradition.* Cambridge: Harvard University Press.

Assie-Lumumba, N'dri T. 2006. *Higher education in Africa. Crises, reforms and transformation.* Working paper series. Dakar: Council for the Development of Social Science Research in Africa.

Benneh, George, Mariama Awumbila, and Paul Effah. 2004. *African universities, the private sector and civil society, forging partnerships for development.* Accra: African Regional Council of the International Association of University Presidents.

Carnegie, Andrew. 1889. *The gospel of wealth.* Reproduced in O'Connell, Brian (ed.). 1983. *America's voluntary spirit.* New York: The Foundation Center.

Cheit Earl, F., and T.E. Lobman. 1979. *Foundations and higher education: Grant-making from golden years through steady state.* Berkeley: Carnegie Council on Policy Studies in Higher Education.

Cloete et al. 2006. *Transformation in higher education—Global pressures and local realities,* Higher Education Dynamics, vol. 10. Dordrecht: Springer.

Coone, Horace. 1990. *Money to Burn. Great American Foundations and Their Money.* Originally published in 1938 by Longmans, Green, and Co. New Brunswick: Transaction Publishers.

Coleman, James S., and David Court. 1993. *University development in the third world. The Rockefeller foundation experience.* Oxford: Pergamon.

Condliffe Lagemann, Ellen. 1983. *Private power for the public good. A history of the Carnegie foundation for the advancement of teaching.* Middleton: Wesleyan University Press.

Curti, Merle. 1963. *American philanthropy abroad. A history.* New Brunswick: Rutgers University Press.

Curti, Merle, and Roderick Nash. 1965. *Philanthropy in the shaping of American higher education.* New Brunswick: Rutgers University Press.

Dowie, Mark. 2002. *American foundations: An investigative history*. Cambridge: MIT Press.

Gray, George W. 1941. *Education on an international scale: A history of the international education board, 1923–1938*. New York: Harcourt, Brace and Company.

Hammack, David C., and Helmut K. Anheier (eds.). 2010. *American foundations. Roles and contributions*. Washington, DC: Brookings Institution Press.

Hollis, Ernerst V. 1938. *Philanthropic foundations and higher education*. New York: Columbia University Press.

Keppel, Frederick P., and James Bertram. 1927. *Report of the President and Secretary as to an Educational Program in Africa*, December 1.

Lulat, Y.G.-M. 2005. *A history of African higher education from antiquity to the present. A critical synthesis*. Westport: Praeger.

Mamdani, Mahmood. 2012. *Reading Ibn Khaldun in Kampala*. Makerere Institute of Social Research Working Paper No. 10, August.

Mamdani, Mahmood, and Mamadou Diouf (eds.). 1994. *Academic freedom in Africa*. Dakar: CODESRIA.

Nielsen, Waldemar A. 1996. *Inside American philanthropy: The dramas of donorship*. Norman: University of Oklahoma Press.

O'Connell, Brian. 1987. *Philanthropy in action*. New York: Foundation Center.

Samoff, Joel, and Bidemi Carrol. 2004. The promise of partnership and continuities of dependence: External support to higher education in Africa. *African Studies Review* 47(1): 67–199.

Whyte, Anne. 2004. *Landscape analysis of donor trends in international development by human and institutional capacity building*. A Rockefeller Foundation series, vol. 2. The Rockefeller Foundation, New York.

Wormser, René. 1958. *Foundations: Their power and influence*. New York: The Devin-Adair Company.

Zeleza, Paul Tiyambe, and Adebayo Olukoshi. 2004. *African universities in the twenty-first century*, vol. 2. Dakar: Council for the Development of Social Science Research in Africa.

CHAPTER 3

Educational Philanthropists and Higher Education Developers

Africa's ecology of donors is composed of numerous international agencies, development funds, international foundations, and pan-African organizations. Together, they form a heterogeneous environment in which all funding decisions are made with a watchful eye as each funder considers the actions of its counterparts, although there are no clear collaborative systems in place among donors. This reality raises important questions about the strategic choices made by donors and the repartition of funds across the continent, as resource-dependent institutions are inherently implicated in the competition for funding. For instance, do contemporary funders establish their strategies based on certain linguistic or colonial lines? Do they follow certain trends in new funding areas, changing direction uniformly with each fad? In order to shed some light on these issues, this chapter examines the grantmaking behavior of US foundations that made grants to institutions in Africa between 2003 and 2013. By the beginning of the new millennium, the institutional demography of African higher education was undergoing marked change and new forms of demand. At the same time, relations among and between institutions and government were evolving in unpredictable ways. African universities emerged as critical engines for socio-economic development in Africa (Assie-Lumumba 2006; Zeleza and Olukoshi 2004; Afolayan 2007). They became integral to the international community of donors and of US foundations in particular, who saw a strategic opportunity to positively impact these institutions on the African continent. Developing the field of higher education toward the promises of knowledge economies meant creating lasting bonds with the future leaders and entrepreneurs of Africa. However, poor collaboration and coordination among donors—particularly among governmental institutions, development agencies, and international organizations—has always been a characteristic of the ecology of higher education development in Africa (Wield 1997).

In 2000, under the impetus of Dr. Vartan Gregorian, President of Carnegie Corporation of New York, the Partnership for Higher Education in Africa

© The Editor(s) (if applicable) and The Author(s) 2016
F. Jaumont, *Unequal Partners*, Philanthropy and Education,
DOI 10.1057/978-1-137-59348-1_3

(PHEA) was launched as a joint effort of the Carnegie Corporation of New York, Ford Foundation, John D. and Catherine T. MacArthur Foundation, The Rockefeller Foundation, to support the capacity building of universities and the field of higher education in Africa. The William and Flora Hewlett Foundation, The Andrew W. Mellon Foundation and The Kresge Foundation were later additions to the Partnership. In launching PHEA, the presidents of the four founding foundations sought to dispel the commonly accepted view that higher education was not a priority and that donors should focus on primary education. The partner foundations contributed close to $440,000,000 in 10 years to build core capacity and support special initiatives at universities in several African countries. Each of the foundations had significant grantmaking programs in Africa prior to forming the Partnership, and continued their activities after the Partnership was terminated in 2010. The PHEA's configuration also suggests that collaboration was a complex matter among private foundations. The issue of inefficient donor collaboration and coordination raises questions about the competing strategies of international donors and private foundations. However, it is necessary to emphasize the complexity of the field of higher education in Africa which can hardly be seen as a uniform system; a one-size-fits-all approach would be very unlikely to succeed.

Moreover, questions of dependence on donor funding arise, particularly when a system is not functioning well, as Samoff and Carroll (2004) state: "In our view, external support to higher education in Africa in general and partnerships in particular can and do play a prominent role in the perpetuation of dependence, and, through the dependence of higher education, in the perpetuation of poverty in Africa."[1] Following Samoff and Carroll's view, the risk of negatively impacting higher education in Africa is high, as is the desire to reach sustainability for all those concerned. Arguably, these active participants are prepared to hold any international developer accountable in the field of higher education in Africa. This chapter narrows its focus on independent foundations in the USA and on the specific sector of higher education in Africa. It is primarily concerned with the relationships between the Partnership's foundations and their field, as well as the foundations' interactions with African universities and academic network.

Considering the scale and complexity of the Partnership's objectives, and the innumerable organizations and programs that were impacted by the foundations' individual and collective choices, the following sections closely examines the Partnership's actions and role in the ecology of higher education development in Africa. It surveys and compares, both quantitatively and qualitatively, the date of their grants and participants. According to the grant database maintained by the Foundation Center in New York City, American philanthropies made 13,565 grants to Africa between 2003 and 2013. All sectors included, 330 US private foundations made grants totaling $3.9 billion to support numerous initiative in Africa. Grant distribution per sector showed a high concentration in agriculture, health, higher education, and research. The higher education sector alone accounts for 25 % of grant receipts. Many African universities, research centers, and higher education networks play an important role in US foundations' overall grantmaking strategies in Africa. Foundations used universities, research centers, and other higher education organizations as receptacles for their grants to fund specific projects in the country or region. For instance, several foundation-funded programs in agriculture, health, or civil rights have created a new position for universities. For instance, the Kenya-based Alliance for a Green Revolution in Africa (AGRA) stands out as the African organization that received the largest grants that any African organization has ever received from US foundations. It received very large grants from Bill and Melinda Gates Foundation and The Rockefeller Foundation. A closer look at AGRA's grant activities shows that many universities are involved in its Education for African Crop Improvement program. They have received significant grants through what could be seen as "re-granting with an African perspective." For instance, the University of KwaZulu-Natal in South Africa received a 4-year grant of $8,069,016 in 2007 to "enable the African Centre for Crop Improvement (ACCI) to continue training young scientists from eastern and southern Africa in crop improvement and to collaborate with other breeding programs in sub-Saharan Africa." The University of Ghana received a 5-year grant of $4,922,752 in 2007 to "establish a West Africa Centre for Crop Improvement (WACCI) at the University of Ghana, Legon." Makerere University in Uganda received a 2-year grant of $400, 000 in 2008 to "ensure production of improved crop varieties adapted to poor farmer conditions through advanced training for a Master of Science in Plant Breeding for ten Ugandan and Rwandan nationals and to strengthen the Plant Breeding research program through the establishment of required facilities at Makerere University."[2] Out of all grants made by US foundations to African institutions between 2003 and 2013, all sectors included, it is clear that universities, research centers, and academic networks were partners of choice for US foundations. Several universities are among the top recipients, particularly South African universities which dominate the table—the University of Cape Town being the most successful recipient of foundation grants by far. Recipients include the University of the Witwatersrand, the University of the Western Cape, the University of KwaZulu-Natal, the University of Pretoria, Rhodes University, and the University of the Stellenbosch. Other universities included Makerere University in Uganda, the American University of Cairo and Cairo University in Egypt, the University of Ghana, and the University of Nairobi. Other types of higher education organizations which received foundation support included research centers such as the African Population and Health Research Center, the Human Sciences Research Council, and the South African Institute for Advancement. Academic networks included the African Economic Research Consortium, the Association of African Universities, among others. It countenances the emergence of African universities and higher education organizations, in the eyes of US grantmakers, as active participants in the development of Africa's knowledge societies. While this study reflects the presence of several universities as top recipients of foundation grants, all sectors included, the survey also found an impressive number of higher education organizations among the grantees of US foundations. Indeed, between 2003 and 2013, 194 recipients classified Scores of universities and higher education institutions in Africa received grants from US foundations since 2000.[3]

One important factor affecting a country's ability to attract grants is its official or primary language. While there are more Francophone countries than Anglophone, Lusophone, and Arabic-speaking countries in Africa, most funding from US foundations went to countries where English is the dominant language. Research shows that foundations demonstrate a tendency to mainly make grants to English-speaking institutions. These findings suggest that US foundations applied a geopolitical strategy of investment and maximized their resources along former colonial lines, particularly favoring former British colonies. US foundations' geopolitical agenda might not be formulated with specific post-colonial considerations. Nonetheless, colonial lines emerge as clear demarcations between Africa's new knowledge societies, and these lines are reinforced by the foundations' grantmaking strategies. The field of higher education development in Africa can be described along these lines. Higher education in Africa in the early 2000s was characterized by a small number of universities per country and low enrollment ratios at all levels. Higher education was experiencing the lack of a clearly defined institutional field. The sector was plagued by challenges such as an aging faculty and lack of incentives to attract younger staff. The issue of a continued brain drain tendency, that afflicts most African countries, was pervasive. Meanwhile, government and businesses provide inadequate financial and logistical support to universities and research centers, thus hindering institutional development.

These beneficiaries included universities and higher education institutions, research centers, academic organizations, and scholarship funds (Table 3.1). The domination of South African universities in the top of the list is clear. So is the number of institutions which use English as the dominant language. With rare exceptions, US foundations made grants to universities, research centers, and academic networks which tended to be located in current or former Commonwealth countries. Francophone countries were poorly represented with the exception of Senegal, Madagascar, and Burkina Faso which received a few grants. Mozambique stood out as an exception in Lusophone Countries. In Arabophone countries, Egypt stood out as an exception, largely due to the presence of the Ford Foundation and the American University in Cairo. Foundations and foundation grants concentrated in South Africa which received 54 % of the total amount of grants and attracted three to four times more US donors than four top recipient countries on the list (Uganda, Nigeria, Ghana, and Kenya). Commonwealth countries dominate the list with 16 countries out of 28, and 8 countries out of the top 10.

More importantly, Commonwealth countries received 93.1 % of the total dollar amount of US foundation grants and 89.6 % of all grants. Commonwealth grantees represented 79.9 % of all US foundations higher education beneficiaries in Africa. This trend is also reflected in the Partnership

Table 3.1   Top US Foundation beneficiaries in higher education in Africa (2003–2013)

Top University Recipients	Country	Grant Total	Main Donor(s)
University of Cape Town	South Africa	$80,902,000	Gates, Carnegie, Atlantic, Mellon
University of the Witwatersrand	South Africa	$49,295,000	Gates, Carnegie Corporation of New York (CCNY), Mellon
University of the Western Cape	South Africa	$47,352,000	Kresge, Atlantic, Mellon, Ford
Makerere University	Uganda	$42,512,000	Rockefeller, Carnegie
University of Kwazulu-Natal	South Africa	$28,742,000	Carnegie, Mellon, Rockefeller
University of Ghana	Ghana	$19,992,000	Gates, Carnegie, Hewlett, Ford
University of Pretoria	South Africa	$19,890,000	Gates, Kellogg, Carnegie, Mellon
University of Zimbabwe	Zimbabwe	$17,154,000	Rockefeller, Kellogg
University of Ibadan	Nigeria	$14,162,000	MacArthur, Ford
University of Dar es Salaam	Tanzania	$12,055,000	Carnegie, Ford, Rockefeller
Rhodes University	South Africa	$10,867,000	Mellon, Atlantic, Kresge, Ford
University of Stellenbosch	South Africa	$10,123,000	Gates, Mellon, Carnegie
Ahmadu Bello University	Nigeria	$8,563,000	MacArthur, Carnegie
American University in Cairo	Egypt	$8,036,000	Ford, Gates, Hewlett
African Virtual University	Kenya	$7,881,000	Ford, MacArthur, Carnegie Rockefeller, Hewlett
Bayero University	Nigeria	$7,158,000	MacArthur
Obafemi Awolowo University	Nigeria	$7,000,000	Carnegie
Cheikh Anta Diop University	Senegal	$6,780,000	Gates
Cairo University	Egypt	$6,614,000	Ford, Mellon
University of Jos	Nigeria	$6,300,000	Carnegie

for Higher Education's overall funding to higher education between 2000 and 2010. Although the Partnership sought to specifically target countries where they always traditionally operated, its funding was mostly distributed to English-speaking institutions in current or former Commonwealth countries. Apart from making grants to former Commonwealth countries, 68 % of the Partnership's dollar contribution targeted nine countries directly for a total of $297.7 million and 899 grants. The remaining 32 % of funds, $142.2 million, and 583 grants were spread across several countries or regions. With $123.8 million and 455 grants, South Africa was by far the country that received most of the Partnership's attention, followed by Nigeria and Uganda. However, considering the differences between each country's Gross Domestic Product (GDP), the dollar amounts indicated in Table 3.1 should be interpreted relatively, taking into account each country's economic factors such as the cost of living. Similarly, the number of grants made per country reflects the capacities of each country's institutions to receive grants. Excluding Uganda, the overall spending of the Partnership was insignificant compared to each government's estimated yearly spending on higher education. When taking into account the relatively minimal funding, the Partnership's enormous visibility during this period reveals far more about the foundations' impressive public relation skills than the size of their contributions. The Partnership also tended to invest more in countries that invested the most themselves in national higher education. The foundations gained access to countries of geopolitical importance through the angle of higher education. They hoped to influence them and others on the continent by participating in the institutionalization of African higher education. Considering that an investment to higher education raises a country's GDP by 5.5 %, whereas an investment to primary education raises it by 1.1 %, as a World Bank report indicates, the Partnership's investments were geared toward maximizing returns on Africa's political and economic potential.[4]

A more extensive survey of US foundations confirms the foundations' general tendency to mainly make grants to English-speaking countries. This finding confirms that US foundations applied a geopolitical strategy of investment maximization along former colonial lines, in particular former British colonies. The following map illustrates this point. It also highlights the Partnership's target countries and marks the foundations' field offices (Fig. 3.1).

By favoring higher education organizations that use English as the language of internal and external communication and learning, US foundations create durable connections with the continent's future leaders and entrepreneurs along a language associated with cultural references that they dominate. Ford Foundation in Egypt is an exception to this rule and is explained by Dr. Dina El'Khawaga in post-colonial terms:

> For the steering committee, Africa was sub-Saharan Africa and not all Africa. The Ford Foundation leadership was kind enough with my ideas that Ford would provide funds for Egypt because of the Partnership. My main point was that these are colonial divisions, you know; let's go with Anglophone Africa and not with Francophone Africa. Let's go with sub-Saharan Africa verses North Africa. And, that we don't really endorse such divisions which were really colonial lines. [5]

Ford Foundation geopolitical agenda might not have been formulated with specific post-colonial considerations. Nonetheless, the colonial lines described above emerge as clear demarcations between Africa's new knowledge societies. These lines are then reinforced by US foundations' grantmaking strategies. Furthermore, from 2003 to 2007, all sectors included, 579 US private foundations made grants totaling $2.1 billion to support numerous initiatives in Africa. Cumulative grants to Africa increased steadily in size and in quantity during this 4-year period. Grant distribution per sector showed a high concentration in agriculture (31 %), health (26 %), and higher education and research (19 %). The geopolitical distribution of these grants confirms the concentration of funds in Commonwealth countries, as described above. Moreover, 50 % of all funding went to three countries: Kenya (22 %), South Africa (19 %), and

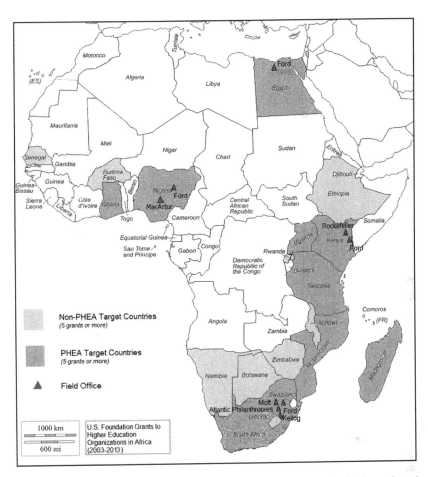

Fig. 3.1 Map of US Foundation countries of focus in Africa for higher education development

Nigeria (11 %)—countries which are not only close to the USA's interests but also very influential on the continent.

The share of foundation grants to higher education in sub-Saharan Africa is possibly higher than these results show since many foundations ran major programs in the sectors of agriculture, health, and development either directly through African universities or indirectly through re-granting intermediaries, research centers and universities in developing countries, or regional non-governmental organizations and foundations. In this light, African universities appear to emerge as critical engines for the socio-economic development of Africa. Thus, viewing them as integral parts in the geopolitical strategies of international donors in general, and of US foundations in particular, makes much sense. In total, 98 foundations were found to have invested in higher education institutions in Africa between 2003 and 2013. These foundations made grants to African higher education that amounted to an estimate of $600 million. Overall, more than 2000 grants were made to 194 higher education institutions in 29 countries in Africa during 2003 and 2013.[6] By comparison, the World Bank's lending for higher education in Sub-Saharan countries amounted to $555.9 million[7] between 1998 and 2008, while United States Agency for International Development (USAID) disbursed an estimate of $350 million; the Swedish International Development Agency (SIPA) approximately $100 million[8], and the British Council disbursed an estimated $50 million during the same period. There were many other players in the field: The International Development Research Centre (IDRC) from Canada; The Canadian International Development Agency (CIDA); the Norwegian Ministry of Foreign Affairs; the Danish Agency for International Development (DANIDA); the United Nations Development Program; the Netherlands Ministry of Foreign Affairs, the Prince Claus Fund among others. Considering the ecology of donors active in African higher education, US foundations appear to be significant players indeed.

Few foundations have offices in Africa. Ford Foundation has offices in Johannesburg, South Africa and Cairo, Egypt. The Rockefeller Foundation has an office in Nairobi, Kenya. John D. and Catherine T. MacArthur Foundation has an office in Abuja, Nigeria. Charles Stewart Mott Foundation and Atlantic Philanthropies have offices in Johannesburg, South Africa. Kellogg had an office in Pretoria, South Africa but closed it in 2009. Other foundations such as Carnegie Corporation of New York, Bill and Melinda Gates Foundation, The Andrew W. Mellon Foundation, The William and Flora Hewlett Foundation, The Kresge Foundation, The David and Lucile Packard Foundation, The McKnight Foundation, among others, operate their Africa programs from their headquarters in the USA and keep an extensive network of representatives in African institutions, many of whom are former academics, researchers or university leaders. The following table shows the largest US grantmakers in the field of higher education in Africa during the same period, the total amount of grants that they made to higher education institutions in Africa, the number of grants and the grant average. The foundations, half of which are located in New York and California, are classified under five main categories in the US Internal Revenue Code: independent foundations; corporate foundations; community foundations; operating foundations; and public charities.[9] US independent or private foundations are the largest, and sometimes most generous types of grantmaking institutions in the field of African higher education. Also known as family foundations, general purpose foundations, special purpose foundations, or private non-operating foundations, independent foundations are organizations that typically have a single major source of funding—usually gifts from one family or corporation rather than funding from many sources. Their primary activity is to make grants to other charitable organizations and to individuals, rather than the direct operation of charitable programs (Cafardi et al. 2006). Corporate foundations are the second most important type of philanthropic organizations found in the field of African higher education. These foundations are usually started by a company, with a single gift that can become the endowment. The company can contribute to this in the future, as it wishes. The foundation's

Table 3.2 Top US Grantmakers to African higher education organizations (2003–2013)

Foundations	State	Number of grants	Total grant amounts	Grant average	PHEA
Ford Foundation	NY	421	$78,826,023	$187,235	✓
Rockefeller Foundation	NY	186	$54,522,589	$293,132	✓
Andrew Foundation	NY	180	$59,791,320	$332,174	✓
Carnegie Corporation of New York	NY	140	$105,278,596	$751,990	✓
John D. and Catherine T. MacArthur Foundation	IL	78	$43,987,054	$563,937	✓
W.K. Kellogg Foundation	MI	58	$42,430,576	$731,562	
Kresge Foundation	MI	49	$21,902,283	$446,985	✓
Atlantic Philanthropies	NY	45	$58,826,876	$1,307,264	
Charles Stewart Mott Foundation	MI	41	$3,751,800	$91,507	
Bill & Melinda Gates Foundation	WA	40	$73,690,156	$1,842,254	
William and Flora Hewlett Foundation	CA	30	$9,433,500	$314,450	✓
Rockefeller Brothers Fund, Inc.	NY	26	$2,016,500	$77,558	
McKnight Foundation	MN	18	$3,223,000	$179,056	
Bristol-Myers Squibb Foundation, Inc.	NY	15	$1,432,002	$95,467	
Citi Foundation	NY	9	$556,100	$61,789	
Spencer Foundation	IL	7	$795,000	$113,571	
Christensen Fund	CA	6	$261,000	$43,500	
Motorola Solutions Foundation	IL	6	$261,000	$43,500	
J. Paul Getty Trust	CA	5	$568,800	$113,760	
Goldman Sachs Foundation	NY	4	$1,550,041	$387,510	
David and Lucile Packard Foundation	CA	4	$599,785	$149,946	
Marin Community Foundation	CA	4	$195,560	$48,890	
Flora Family Foundation	CA	4	$180,000	$45,000	
Western Union Foundation	CO	4	$140,000	$35,000	
Starr Foundation	NY	4	$100,000	$25,000	
Oprah Winfrey Foundation	IL	3	$1,300,000	$433,333	
Doris Duke Charitable Foundation	NY	3	$570,500	$190,167	
JPMorgan Chase Foundation	NY	3	$216,000	$72,000	
Alfred P. Sloan Foundation	NY	3	$128,000	$42,667	
Google.org	CA	2	$1,250,000	$625,000	
Charles A. Dana Foundation, Inc.	NY	2	$557,002	$278,501	
GE Foundation	CT	2	$200,000	$100,000	
Silicon Valley Community Foundation	CA	2	$200,000	$100,000	
Levi Strauss Foundation	CA	2	$129,000	$64,500	
Michael and Susan Dell Foundation	TX	2	$122,132	$61,066	

officers are usually the company's owners and key executives. Company-sponsored foundations such as The Bristol-Myers Squibb Foundation, The Goldman Sachs Foundation, Citi Foundation, Motorola Solutions Foundation, GE Foundation, The JPMorgan Chase Foundation, The Coca-Cola Foundation, Google.org, among others, have made grants to Africa in the areas of health, education, research, and economic development (Table 3.2).

Community foundations are public charities that conduct grantmaking activities which often, but not always, benefit local charities and charitable community projects. Generally, community foundations do not operate their own programs. Examples include Silicon Valley Community Foundation, Marin Community Foundation, The Pittsburgh Foundation, and New York Community Trust. The fourth type is operating foundations. These private foundations may make grants, but the amount of grants generally awarded is small relative to the funds used for the foundation's own programs. Operating foundations such as The Oprah Winfrey Foundation devote most of their resources to their programs and activities. Finally, public charities are also important grantmakers in Africa, though not necessarily through grants to higher education institutions. They can be a religion-affiliated funder such as Samaritan's Purse or a medical research organization operated in conjunction with a hospital such as Howard Hughes Medical Institute.

While focusing on the development of higher education as a whole in Africa foundations focused on a number of specific areas in target universities. For the sake of clarity, these areas are classified along the following four categories: "Access," which included scholarship funds and financial aid; "Capacity Building," which included management development, operating support, endowments, buildings and renovation, and technology; "Branches of Learning," which included Curriculum development, program evaluation, faculty and staff development, and research; and "Dissemination," which included conferences, publication, exhibitions, and advocacy. The following figure offers an illustration of foundation grant distribution in African higher education. They summarize the organization of programmatic activities of 97 US foundations, at the same time indicating funding trends between 2003 and 2013. The seven Partnership foundations accounted for 65.2 % of all dollars invested in higher education in Africa during that time frame and 73.7 % of all grants (Fig. 3.2).

Capacity building dominated the study's sample. While more dollars were attributed to capacity building, more grants served branches of knowledge. Partnership foundations mainly focused on capacity building, although not as much as the other foundations. Partnership foundations prioritized creating access more so than other foundations. Capacity building became a popular mode of operation for US foundations. It also suggests that the Partnership might have played a role in endorsing this mode across the ecology of US foundations involved with African higher education. Furthermore, the data confirms that most foundations do not play a role in promoting social change and

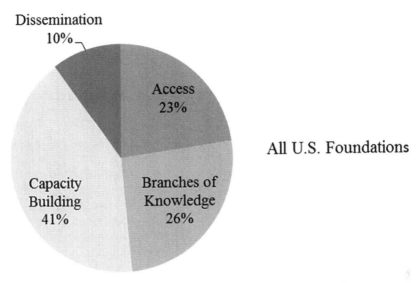

Fig. 3.2   Comparison of foundation funding to higher education in Africa per category

greater opportunities for underserved populations. The Access line indicates that most giving served the purposes of providing broad institutional support, just as foundations have done for decades in the USA. Similar to their actions in the realm of US higher education, foundations as a whole appear content to meet the core capacity and capital needs of higher education, rather than to push these institutions to change and ready themselves for major access issues that confront the field.

LANGUAGE BIAS AND GRANTMAKING IN AFRICA

As the mechanisms of international grantmaking and foreign investment are extremely complex, all grantmaking decisions are made in a handful of dominant languages, which are for the most part European and tied to the continent's colonial history. This reality raises important questions about the influence of languages on the distribution of funds across the continent. As resource-dependent institutions compete for funds, their respective dominant languages can serve as indicators of success in the quest for external funds. This phenomenon continues to hold significance today as English continues to spread and assert its position as the dominant international language. It is also relevant to understand the habits of funders, particularly if certain biases exist toward institutions that speak a preferred language. The geopolitical distribution of US foundation grants suggests that they show a preference for countries where English is widely spoken or where English is an official language.

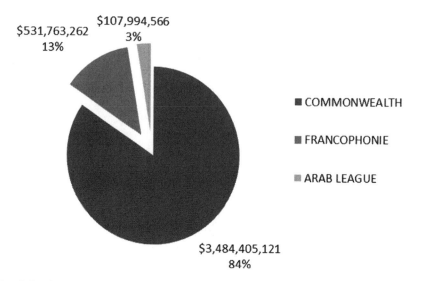

Fig. 3.3   Comparison of foundation funding by linguistic group

Sixty-eight percent of all funding went to three countries: South Africa (30 %), Kenya (29 %), and Nigeria (9 %). These predominantly English-speaking countries are not only close to the USA's interest but also among the most influential on the continent in terms of their economic and political weight. The three most widely-spoken languages in Africa by geographical area and total number of speakers are English, Arabic, and French. These languages, which are often the dominant language of politics and business, correspond to three geopolitical groups: the Commonwealth of Nations, the League of Arab Nations, and the Organisation Internationale de la Francophonie (OIF) (Fig. 3.3). The graph below lists the member of each organization and the total amount in grants they received from US foundations between 2003 and 2013.[10]

Grants were not allocated evenly across these language groups. French-speaking and Arab-speaking countries did not receive much support from US foundations, with the exception of Senegal, Madagascar, and Burkina Faso. With a share of grant receipts of 84 %, Commonwealth countries received a vast majority of grants authorized between 2003 and 2013. Moreover, while there are more Francophone countries than any other language block, both by number of countries and total number of speakers, most funding from US foundations went to countries where English is the dominant language. Although Francophone countries received a notable percentage of grants (13 %), this is not representative of the relative number, size, or population of these countries. While 31 African countries belong to the OIF, only $531,763,262 was allocated to its members by US grantmakers between 2003 and 2013, whereas the 19 countries belonging to the Commonwealth of Nations received $3,484,405,121. Because the force of cultural influence plays such an important role in the development of the African continent, and the competition between international languages within a knowledge economy represents a struggle between rival modes of development (particularly in a university setting), these figures confirm a definite advantage for English-language institutions. In Arab-speaking countries, Egypt was the only recipient of foundation grants, largely due to the presence of Ford Foundation which has an office in Cairo that has provided funds to a number of higher education institutions and non-governmental organizations. Foundations grants were concentrated in South Africa, which received 54 % of the total amount of grants and attracted three to four times more US donors than four top recipient countries on the list (Uganda, Nigeria, Ghana, and Kenya). [11] More importantly, Commonwealth grantees represented 79.9 % of all US foundations higher education beneficiaries in Africa.[12] This trend is also reflected in the Partnership for Higher Education's overall funding to higher education between 2000 and 2010. Although the Partnership sought to specifically target countries where they traditionally operated, or where they had already built strong relationships with universities and academic networks, funding was mostly distributed to English-speaking institutions in current or former Commonwealth countries. In addition, this pattern is remarkably consistent across years and foundations, as illustrated in the graphs below. Every one of the top ten US foundations made out at least 80 % of its grants to countries within the Commonwealth of Nations. For Ford Foundation, The Andrew W. Mellon Foundation, The Coca-Cola Foundation, this number is close to 100 %. This overwhelmingly clear pattern confirms that the primary language of grant recipients played a central role in the ecology of grantmaking in Africa, particularly among US foundations (Fig. 3.4).

Foundations' preference for English is particularly evident in the field of higher education. In total, this study identified 97 foundations that invested $573.5 million in higher education organizations in Africa between 2003 and 2013. During that time frame, more than 2000 grants were made to 194 higher education institutions in 29 countries. Within the context of higher education, a country's official medium of instruction, or the language that is used in classes and to complete assignments, represents an important but complex factor: In many countries, the medium of instruction varies between primary, secondary, and tertiary schools. As expected, US foundations have invested in higher education on the African continent, targeting institutions where English was the primary medium of instruction. More than 90 % of higher education institutions that received grants from US foundations listed English as the primary medium of instruction compared to 4 % for French and 3 % for Arabic.[13]

Furthermore, in addition to higher education institutions, the share of foundation grants to higher education in sub-Saharan Africa also included major foundation-supported programs in agriculture, health, and development. In this light, universities contributed significantly to the socio-economic development of the African continent by producing knowledge, skills, and innovations relevant to African contexts. Thus, viewing universities as "engines of development"

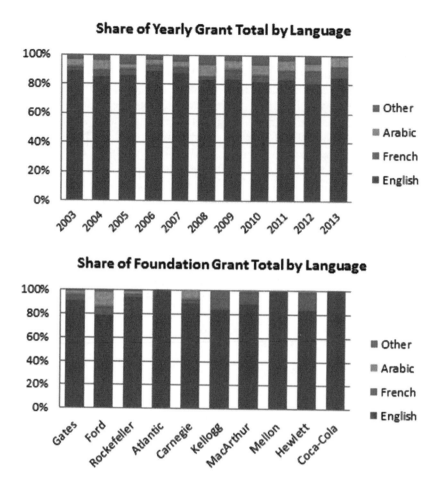

Fig 3.4   Share of yearly & foundation grant total by language

or, in other words, as integral parts of Africa's economic future reflects various geopolitical strategies valued by international donors and, particularly, US foundations.

These strategies, however, need to take careful account of the different organizational structures that prevail among African higher education institutions according to their location in countries where Arabic, English, French, or Portuguese are spoken. The following excerpt is from an interview with Andrea Johnson, program officer at Carnegie Corporation of New York:

The francophone countries had universities organized on the French model, which is very different from the British model and the Lusophone model. That's partly too why Mozambique was problematic. They weren't organized the same way. So where as you can have conversations across the Anglophone universities...it's not even the language barrier, it's deeper than that.[14]

The PHEA presents an interesting case study for the relationship between US foundations and African Universities, especially in relation to the question of the primary medium of instruction. The Partnership provided most of its funding to higher education institutions in seven English-dominant African nations: Ghana, Kenya, Nigeria, South Africa, Tanzania, and Uganda. Institutions in Mozambique, Egypt, and Madagascar were added to the list of grant recipients. The foundations' involvement with higher education networks could have indirectly served the academic community of the continent, particularly through university connectivity, including non-English-speaking institutions, although this was not the Partnership's immediate objective.

However, a small minority of non-English institutions did receive funding from US foundations. Between 2003 and 2013, US foundations made 217 grants to higher education institutions in countries where English is not the primary medium of instruction, totaling $81,211,150. Universities and research institutions that listed Arabic as their medium of instruction received 129 grants totaling $31,181,657, those that listed French received 70 grants totaling $40,599,438, and those that listed Portuguese received only 17 grants totaling $6,442,148. The following table details the specifics of grants awarded to institutions with non-English mediums of instruction in Africa (Table 3.3).

Ford Foundation behavior is particularly remarkable when considering the importance of language on grantmaking. The Foundation was the top donor for every non-English medium of instruction sector (excluding Portuguese); 35 % of Ford's grants targeting higher education in Africa were given to universities and research institutions that did not use English as their primary medium of instruction. However, these grants were not equally distributed.

Another important factor impacting a country's ability to attract grants is its official language. While there are more African Francophone countries than Anglophone, Lusophone, and Arabophone countries, most funding from US foundations went to countries where English is the dominant language. This finding confirms foundations' general tendency to favor English-speaking institutions and suggests that US foundations tend to make grants along former colonial lines, particularly to former British colonies. Although the geopolitical agendas of US foundations may not be formulated with specific post-colonial considerations, colonial lines emerge as clear demarcations between Africa's new knowledge societies. These lines are reinforced by the foundations' grantmaking strategies.

The discourse on priorities in African higher education is placed in a contested terrain. Grantmakers must contend with inhospitable national contexts that often hamper their desire to invest in grantees that need the most support. This is exacerbated when foundations face a language barrier with a prospective grantee. As such, US foundations tend not to engage sufficiently with non-English-speaking institutions, even when said institutions would benefit the most from their support. Instead, US foundations concentrated their efforts on a select number of Anglophone institutions. These were, for the most part, elite institutions to which foundations were accustomed to giving

Table 3.3 Grants to institutions with non-English mediums of instruction in Africa

French		Arabic		Portuguese	
Foundation	Total	Foundation	Total	Foundation	Total
Ford	$19,558,939	Ford	$23,243,293	W.K. Kellogg	$3,231,000
Bill & Melinda Gates	$6,947,956	UN Women's Fund for Gender Equality	$2,592,000	Ford	$2,825,748
The John D. and Catherine T. MacArthur	$5,022,670	Carnegie Corporation of New York	$2,130,000	Gilead	$ 124,200
Carnegie Corporation of New York	$2,882,825	Open Society Institute	$1,071,315	The Rockefeller	$ 104,400
The William and Flora Hewlett	$2,499,920	The William and Flora Hewlett	$867,000	Bill & Melinda Gates	$ 101,000
The Bristol-Myers Squibb, Inc.	$ 1,239,320	Bill & Melinda Gates	$404,793	Engineering Information	$ 55,800
Open Society Institute	$534,775	Avon for Women	$179,850		
The Rockefeller	$521,381	The Charles A. Dana, Inc.	$151,380		
J. Paul Getty Trust	$473,800	The Bodman	$104,500		
Wallace Global Fund II	$150,362	Western Union	$100,200		
Humanity United	$150,362	Foundation to Promote Open Society	$83,003		
The McKnight	$129,710	Citi	$78,660		
John Templeton	$73,614	J. Paul Getty Trust	$56,064		
The Andrew W. Mellon	$45,200	Rockefeller Brothers Fund, Inc.	$54,000		
National Endowment for Democracy	$40,800	The Andrew W. Mellon	$29,120		
The David and Lucile Packard	$28,250	Alfred P. Sloan	$21,600		
Fund For Global Human Rights, Inc.	$26,750	Johnson & Johnson Family of Companies	$14,880		
Koch, Inc.	$18,000				
W. K. Kellogg	$16,350				
Annenberg	$15,024				
The Global Fund for Women	$11,093				
The J.W.	$1200				

funds. By favoring higher education institutions that used English as the language of internal instruction and external communication, US foundations created robust connections with the continent's future leaders and entrepreneurs in the dominant language, culture, and traditions they were accustomed to. Arguably, the lasting connections established between US foundations and Africa's elite, maintained through the English language, ensure a guaranteed return on investment for donors in English-speaking nations.

This approach of targeted selection, which has remained central to US foundations' strategies of institutional development, is understandable. Yet, it has put many institutions of higher learning at a disadvantage in their attempts to attract foundation funding. Universities in Francophone, Lusophone, and Arabophone countries appear to be less equipped to receive grants from US foundations, along with less prestigious institutions and fields that are not deemed a priority for foundations. Considering the importance of language and culture in the mechanisms of globalization, and acknowledging that language groups compete in the knowledge economy, the influence of US foundations in Africa reinforced the dominance of English as the lingua franca of the continent's development.

NOTES

1. Samoff and Carroll (2004), p. 72.
2. Retrieved in 2008 from the website of AGRA.
3. See Appendix for full list.
4. Bloom et al. (2006).
5. August 16, 2011 phone interview with Dr. Dina El'Khawaga, program officer, Ford Foundation, Egypt.
6. Based on a 09/15, survey of grants reported in the Foundation Center's online directory by US foundations between 2003 and 2013. The search criteria included all countries in Africa and recipient types that included the keywords "higher education; higher education reform; higher education / college; higher education/university." The search did not include non-African grant recipients who collaborate with African higher education or serve as intermediaries between foundations and African higher educations.
7. Between 1998 and 2008, Bank lending for higher education averaged $327 million per year. The Latin America and Caribbean region received the largest share (43 %), followed by the East Asia and Pacific (21 %). The Africa region accounted for 17 %. The South Asia region had 12 %. The Middle East and North Africa region had 9 %. The Europe and Central Asia region received 6 %. Source: The World Bank.
8. Estimate based on SIPA's 2002 and 2005 Facts and Figures Reports on Education.
9. Every organization that qualifies for tax exemption as an organization described in section 501(c)(3) of the Internal Revenue Code is a private foundation unless it falls into one of the categories specifically excluded from that term, such as hospitals or universities and organizations that normally receive a substantial

part of their support from a governmental unit or from the general public. See Cafardi and Fabean (2006).

10. See Appendix D for a complete list of US foundations grant recipients by country and linguistic Groups (Grants made between 2003 and 2013. Source: Foundation Center).

11. Commonwealth countries dominate the list with 16 countries represented out of a total 28, as well as 8 out of the top 10. See Appendix D for a complete list of US foundations grant recipients by country and linguistic Groups (Grants made between 2003 and 2013. Source: Foundation Center).

12. See Appendix E for the Top 50 Higher Education Grant Recipients of US Foundations Funding in Africa. Grants made between 2003 and 2013. Source: Foundation Center.

13. English is the primary language of instruction in Botswana, Cameroon, The Gambia, Kenya, Lesotho, Malawi, Mauritius, Namibia, Nigeria, Rwanda, Sierra Leone, South Africa, Swaziland, Tanzania, Uganda, Zambia, and Zimbabwe.

14. August 10, 2011 interview with Andrea Johnson, Program Officer, Higher Education and Libraries in Africa, International Program, Carnegie Corporation of New York.

Bibliography

Afolayan, Michael O. 2007. *Higher education in postcolonial Africa: Paradigms of development, decline, and dilemmas.* Trenton: Africa World Press.

Assie-Lumumba, N'dri T. 2006. *Higher education in Africa. Crises, reforms and transformation.* Working paper series. Dakar: Council for the Development of Social Science Research in Africa.

Benneh, George, Mariama Awumbila, and Paul Effah. 2004. *African universities, the private sector and civil society, forging partnerships for development.* Accra: African Regional Council of the International Association of University Presidents.

Bloom, D., D. Canning, and K. Chan. 2006. *Higher education and economic development in Africa.* Report sponsored by the World Bank.

Cafardi P. Nicholas and Fabean Cherry Jaclyn. 2006. *Understanding Nonprofit and Tax Exempt Organizations.* Newark: LexisNexis.

Samoff, Joel, and Bidemi Carrol. 2004. The promise of partnership and continuities of dependence: External support to higher education in Africa. *African Studies Review* 47(1): 67–199.

Wield, David. 1997. Coordination of donors in African universities. *Higher Education Policy* 10(1): 41–54.

Zeleza, Paul Tiyambe, and Adebayo Olukoshi. 2004. *African universities in the twenty-first century,* vol. 2. Dakar: Council for the Development of Social Science Research in Africa.

PART II

The Commonalities of Philanthropic Foundations

CHAPTER 4

Foundations Come with Institutional Cultures

Foundations are non-material entities shaped by values, norms, habits, and ideas embedded in the institutions themselves. These ideals are internalized by their personnel who behave, bounded by their cultural environment, so as to conform to existing rules or values. As such, foundations are governed by a collection of interrelated rules and routines which determine the way in which actors respond to a given situation. This chapter investigates a partnership between seven major US foundations: Carnegie Corporation of New York, Ford Foundation, John D. and Catherine T. MacArthur Foundation, The Rockefeller Foundation, The William and Flora Hewlett Foundation, The Andrew W. Mellon Foundation, and The Kresge Foundation. In 2000, they formed the PHEA to turn the spotlight of international philanthropy toward the development of higher education in Africa. They sought to strengthen African universities and place them at the center of Africa's economic development. Between 2000 and 2010, the Partnership provided funding to higher education institutions in nine African nations: Ghana, Kenya, Nigeria, Mozambique, South Africa, Tanzania, Uganda, Madagascar, and Egypt. The partnership ended in January 2010 after 10 years and $440 million invested in the field of higher education in Africa. The collaboration between these foundations is largely the product of existing similarities and affinities between them, including a preexisting interest in higher education and African development. The foundations' grantmaking strategies, their wide-ranging interests and their attention to various aspects of higher education on the African continent, and their signature initiatives are examined below. Interestingly, these seven foundations all contributed in varying degrees to the development of US higher education in the nineteenth and early twentieth century. Their experience in higher education at home has modeled their interest in higher education abroad. Within the larger context of higher education developers in Africa, the groundbreaking impact of these foundations' respective endeavors over academic institutions and research networks—accomplished over decades of

© The Editor(s) (if applicable) and The Author(s) 2016
F. Jaumont, *Unequal Partners*, Philanthropy and Education,
DOI 10.1057/978-1-137-59348-1_4

strategic grantmaking both at home and on the African continent—has placed the Partnership's foundations in a league of their own.

INSTITUTIONAL CULTURES VERSUS BUREAUCRATIC PROCESSES

Large foundations are organized around a set of interrelated rules and routines to which their staff respond appropriately. These procedures can be traced back to the origins, historical path, and institutional structure of each foundation. They can also be explained by the different managerial philosophies of foundation leaders. Some foundations may have a decentralized structure, where the president gives general instructions to the staff and allows for a fair amount of autonomy. Others can have a more firmly organized culture in which the president is watchful of the decision-making processes. Similarly, some foundations may prefer to hire leaders and senior staff with strong business-oriented managerial skills, while others might prefer recruiting from within academic circles. Among the foundations examined for this study, most have regularly hired university leaders to become their presidents (as is the case with Carnegie Corporation of New York, The Rockefeller Foundation, John D. and Catherine T. MacArthur Foundation and The Andrew W. Mellon Foundation), while some contrasted this trend by hiring leaders from the corporate world (such as Ford Foundation and The William and Flora Hewlett Foundation). These choices can have an impact on the way a foundation is run and on the strategy it chooses to pursue.

From interviews with foundation staff, it became clear that bureaucratic cultures were sometimes perceived as rigid institutions reminiscent of public administrations. Tade Aina, one of Carnegie's program directors, described the foundations' institutional cultures with the following words: "I think first and foremost the biggest problems we have is that foundations come with their cultures and these traditional cultures can be as rigid as any bureaucracy. In fact, they can almost be beyond, in terms of the rigidities, almost like a culture, it is almost like different princely orders."[1] This view was echoed by Kole Shettima, director of the MacArthur Foundation in Nigeria. He comments:

> We learned some things that we didn't know before, working with other organizations in terms of even their own process of grantmaking, their own processes of decision-making. We appreciated that motivations are different; the way people do some things are different from others. It is not a question of which one is better but it is a question of appreciating and understanding our differences. We are much different also in terms of the image and the perception of the foundations on the [African] continent.[2]

These differences in values and bureaucratic processes played an important part in defining the Partnership's mission, and complicated the Partnership's day-to-day operations. However, they also helped foundation staff learn about their counterparts in other foundations, forcing them to work in a quid pro quo fashion in order to preserve the spirit of collaboration, even if the extent to which that spirit manifested itself fluctuated among certain partners during different stages of the Partnership.

Furthermore, many independent foundations are defined by a charter and governed by a board of trustees, as their respective founders are no longer alive. This contrasts sharply with foundations that have a living donor who can both govern and play an active part in the foundation's day-to-day operations. An example of this would be Bill and Melinda Gates, who are fully engaged in their foundation, participate in governance, and often lend their voice to some of the foundation's key initiatives. The foundations surveyed in this study had no living donors. All had constitutions and bylaws that often dictated each foundation's mission in broad terms in accordance with the founder's general wishes. Joint funding was not achieved easily because of a number of reasons: joint grants required approvals by the board of several foundations and, from a practical point of view, was very time consuming and complicated. This, in part, is why it was not possible for these foundations to have a common fund in order to bankroll joint projects. Moreover, this was inconsistent with the charter of foundations, which spells out its mission and dictates both the foundation's geographic scope and its programmatic focus. For instance, Carnegie Corporation of New York charter restricts its international grantmaking to countries that are or have been in the British Commonwealth.[3] This clearly limits Carnegie's impact to Anglophone countries. However, the foundation has funded specific programs and organizations in non-English speaking-countries (such as the Council for the Development of Social Science Research in Africa in Senegal) as said organizations serve Carnegie's regional interests (in this case, the development of a social science research network on the continent).

Each foundation's constitution is enforced by a board of trustees that appoints the foundation's president and approves strategic orientations. Whether dictated by a charter, imposed by a board, or inherited from decades of foundation history, each foundation's rules and norms influenced the Partnership's overall equilibrium. As such, each Partnership foundation operated with a specific set of rules and grantmaking mechanisms that hindered joint funding strategies. Problems emerged with differences in opinion, projects, and cycles of grantmaking. For example, some foundations offered 3-year grants while others preferred 2-year spans, and some foundations renewed their grants consistently, while others did not consider grant renewals whatsoever.

Comparing these foundations across a number of variables sheds some light on the inner workings of these partnerships. The following table compares the size, grantmaking abilities, and interest in higher education of these seven foundations. The table also details the foundations' date of incorporation, location, size, and rank among US grantmakers. Finally, it lists the foundations' various areas of funding both in Africa and in the field of higher education (Table 4.1)

There are certain historical factors that can help understand the foundations' disposition to work together. Although many foundations including Carnegie Corporation of New York, The Rockefeller Foundation, and Ford Foundation share decades of cooperation in African higher education, these connections

Table 4.1 Comparison between the partnership's seven foundations

	Ford	Hewlett	MacArthur	Mellon	Rockefeller	Kresge	Carnegie
Total assets ($)[1] US rank by asset size[2]	10.5 billion 2nd	7.38 billion 5th	5.67 billion 9th	5.46 billion 11th	3.59 billion 15th	3.1 billion 16th	2.5 billion 20th
Total grants approved ($)	525.9 million	207.1 million	243.77 million	222.2 million	141 million	158 million	96.7 million
Grants awarded Funding to Africa by $[3]	1487 6th	526 8th	455 9th	463 11th	382 2nd	481 15th	210 4th
By number of grants[4]	1st	21st	13th	14th	5th	29th	17th
African Higher Ed. Focus	Since 1950s	Since 1970s	Since 1980s	Since 1990s	Since 1913	Since 1990s	Since 1927
Areas of focus in Africa other than higher education	Economic prospect for communities. Democracy, rights, justice, education, creativity, free expression. Reproductive health.	Development, population policy. Transparency. Education. Think tanks. Reproductive health.	Human rights, international justice. Population, reproductive health.	South Africa initiative. Conservation, environment & the humanities.	Agriculture, climate, environmental & social responsibility; public health. Evaluation practices.	South Africa initiative.	Libraries.
Areas of focus in higher education in the USA and other parts of the world	Advancing higher education access & success.	Open educational resources.	Higher education in Russia.	Higher education scholarship, information technology. Humanities, social sciences. Partnerships.	Philanthropy, poverty, environment, urban innovation, government, transportation. Health. Fine arts.	Higher education productivity. Institutional support. Pathways to college	Higher educated in Eurasia. US urban & higher education.

fluctuate over time. John Butler-Adams, program officer at Ford Foundation's South Africa office, commented on this fluctuation:

> In 2005, Ford's priorities meshed very well with Rockefeller and Carnegie, not so closely with MacArthur. In the second phase, particularly as Rockefeller had a new president who was changing directions, our values and priorities were to a very large extent coincident with those of Carnegie and to a lesser degree but not in any seriously lesser degree with Mellon. And, then when Kresge joined, for the most part, our values and priorities in grantmaking were very similar to those of Kresge.[4]

Indeed, the foundations' willingness to collaborate with each other fluctuated over time depending upon the individuals who lead them. They build connections, and form collaborations, based on values that they may share at a given moment. These values are embedded in the people who serve the foundations, and represent them outside of the institution in meetings, at conferences, or in various communications with the public or with their peers.

There are other important factors that explain the basis of foundation partnerships. Geographic factors, however, are not sufficient to explain these affinities. Indeed, while four of the foundations in this study are headquartered in New York, their respective missions varied greatly. There are important monetary symmetries that help explain the foundations' like-mindedness, beginning with the size of their respective endowments; the seven foundations in the Partnership rank among the 25 largest in the nation. Size matters in the world of foundations and it is clear that each partner's financial assets brought them together. In the PHEA, factors that determined membership included the foundations' track records, longevity, grantmaking strategies, and diverse areas of expertise in Africa and higher education. The Partnership also benefitted from its members' individual name and reputation which, put together, gave the Partnership additional respectability. Moreover, in order to build a strong case for higher education in Africa, the Partnership's foundations had to deliver a clear and convincing message and assert their position among higher education developers. By doing so, they became forceful advocates for the cause of higher education and helped several universities become highly esteemed in their respective national contexts. To a certain extent, the Partnership's respectable image, and the message it delivered, was intricately tied to the foundations' reputations and their place among the credible players of international and human development in Africa. The results produced by the Partnership as a whole reflected well on the individual foundations. This virtuous circle was beneficial to the foundations' work and reinforced their choices in Africa. As such, the connection between affinity and reputation in the Partnership is an important mechanism to explain how collaboration maximized their impact. In examining the seven foundations' size of endowment, cultural adequacy, and interests, there is explicit indication that their impact was maximized through the aggregation of reputation and the association of reputable names: The names of prestigious philanthropic institutions ranked in the top 20 of US foundations, and the names of the major business leaders who gave birth to these foundations. This aggregation of organizations, names, and reputations formed an impressive grantmaking machine designed for high-impact philanthropy. At the dawn of the twenty-first century, these foundations sought to proclaim that higher education in Africa was worthy of large investments and should be an area of interest for the community of donors, education developers, and governments alike.

The differences of foci and approaches within the consortium brought both advantages and challenges to the Partnership. On the one hand, each foundation could offer and gain new perspectives on the field of African higher education. On the other, there was no unified strategy and no clear coordination between partner foundations. For instance, because of its emphasis on reproductive health, the Ford Foundation might have made a grant related to an institution working on the training of professionals in the medical field. Carnegie Corporation of New York, on the other hand, might have been looking to build the capacities of the next generation of academics, including Masters and PhD students working in reproductive rights. Thus, aligning strategically was only possible if it did not disrupt existing initiatives undertaken by the partnering foundations. For instance, Ford's African Higher Education initiatives operated through its regional offices since the early 1990s. The foundation's involvement in African higher education was part of a strategy to strengthen democratic values, reduce poverty and injustice, promote international cooperation, and advance human achievement by working with academic institutions that were located in communities that directly experienced these challenges. Ford's initiatives, which were mainly implemented through grants to individuals, institutions, or agencies working in higher education, played a crucial role in responding to new needs brought about by political and economic changes. When Ford joined the Partnership in 2000, it tried to stay closely aligned to the Partnership while preserving its programs, particularly the African Higher Education Initiative (AHEI) that encompassed grants made by its Middle East and North Africa office and varied somewhat in focal areas and themes. In some ways, the AHEI functioned as a partnership within the larger PHEA Partnership.

Although it maintained a strategic and collaborative alignment, the Partnership expanded individual resources of the foundations by allowing each foundation to make grants according to its own mechanisms, all while identifying grants made to higher education in Africa as Partnership grants. This approach was designed to generate even greater investment in the field of higher education in Africa. Kole Shettima, program director of the MacArthur Foundation's Nigeria office, notes:

> The consortium, at first, was designed to have two purposes. First to demonstrate to Africa that American foundations were really eager to be supportive. The other impact was through a kind of competition to set a total amount of money that would be assured… That would in some sense prod the individual foundations to push as hard as they could in their African support.[5]

Other foundation program officers also observed the positive impact of this competitive-collaborative approach of grantmaking, and on the likelihood of collaboration among foundations. Raoul Davion, program officer for the John D. and Catherine T. MacArthur Foundation, commented, "One dimension was a sense of competitiveness in terms of grant dollars that each foundation could put into [the Partnership], and that served the goal of promoting higher education in Africa well, because the leadership was committed to matching what the other foundations were willing to do."[6] Thus, the hybrid competitive-collaborative approach aided foundations in aligning their focus and pushed them to invest in more grants than they would have otherwise made.

Looking only at large grants, defined as grants greater than $675,000, can help visualize the foundations' overall grantmaking strategies. The following graph illustrates each foundation's individual grantmaking pattern. These patterns reflect the specificity of each funder and their respective financial engagement with the Partnership (Fig. 4.1).

Grants came in many shapes and sizes. Some foundations made larger grants and took greater risks than others. Between 2000 and 2010, Carnegie Corporation of New York, and the John D. and Catherine T. MacArthur Foundation were the most active funders in African higher education in terms of large grants, while Ford Foundation and The Andrew W. Mellon Foundation preferred a small grant approach. This contrast in grantmaking strategy suggests that multiple concurrent approaches were acceptable and that no specific uniformed grant processes were imposed on the Partnership's foundations. Whether the size of the grants reflected the level of trust between grantors and beneficiaries, the efficiency of a foundation's operation, or the level of risk a foundation was willing to take, the Partnership's asymmetrical grant sizes did not affect its equilibrium. Instead, it provided much needed flexibility to accomplish ambitious goals (such as transforming an entire field), while providing

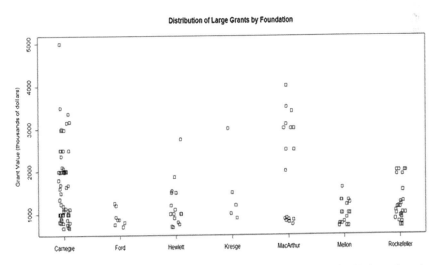

Fig. 4.1 Distribution of large grants by foundation (Partnership for higher education in Africa [2000–2010])

equal veto power among the partners regardless of the amount of money each was willing to commit. The prerogatives of preserving each foundation's institutional singularity forced the Partnership's actors to think creatively. The foundations' lofty ambition to tackle continent-wide issues in the field of higher education in Africa pushed them into establishing a large-scale grantmaking that would foster resource expansion. In practical terms, this was achieved through the addition of individual and joint grants in the Partnership. Moreover, examining the probability of involvement and collaboration among foundations showed that they did not act as united as one would have expected. Instead, they demonstrated a mix of varying levels of cohesion that served their own strategic agendas. Thus, the foundations retained a high degree of individuality which might seem contradictory to the principles of collaboration. The Partnership acted as a confederation with concurrent agendas, interdependent dynamics, and limited joint funding. But, in the case of the PHEA, the sum of its parts was greater than the whole; the foundations' drive to outperform other partners superseded their willingness to work collaboratively.

Foundations within the Partnership also had a tendency to collaborate in smaller groups of preferred partners rather than as a unified group. As was discussed earlier, foundations pursued different grantmaking strategies with respect to their core mission. The reason foundations collaborate may vary. In the case of the Partnership, research shows that, of a total of 1432 grants made between 2000 and 2010, Ford Foundation, Carnegie Corporation of New York, John D. and Catherine T. MacArthur Foundation and The Rockefeller Foundation collaborated with one another the most on joint grants. Their collaboration not only denoted a strong relationship but also a degree of adherence and convergence to the Partnership's ideals. Sharing the same goals, and working toward them, requires shared core values and cultural norms that render collaboration possible and increase its benefits. Knowledge transfer was a clear benefit, and materialized in most exchanges between foundations through reports, meetings, and informal communication. Valuable information was exchanged among partners, and helped reduce risks in grantmaking while increasing efficiency.

The connection between knowledge transfer and efficiency suggests that knowledge sharing was one of the greatest incentives associated with being a member of the Partnership. Indeed, it was a significant motivator for the members involved. Janice Petrovich, former program director at the Ford Foundation, confirms, "The collaborative was very rich in that it was very enlightening to go to these meetings, understand the complexity, and identify those areas that might be difficult to try to work through or how to operate within a difficult environment."[7] The transfer of knowledge between the partners accelerated and expanded opportunities for the foundations. It also multiplied the number of targeted organizations, as David Court, former program officer at The Rockefeller Foundation, indicates:

> It brought a lot of contact with other organizations, it accelerated contact with what others were doing, and initially at least expanded what my ideas about what could possibly and conceivably be done, if the amount of funding was greater,

and the involvement of other organizations and institutions was going to happen. It strengthened my own sense that this needed to be done by quite detailed knowledge about what's happening on the ground, and that it needed to give more emphasis to triumph, involvement and assessment than it had done in the past.[8]

Interviewees also commented on the possible association between the Partnership's knowledge transfer and the expansion of human resources. At Ford, the Partnership inspired the creation of new positions in addition to the existing higher education program officers in New York and in South Africa. When the Partnership ended, positions had been created in Egypt, Kenya, and Nigeria. Other foundations had added staff dedicated to higher education in Africa at their headquarters in the USA. The Partnership had a better coordinating office based out of New York University. Overall, the Partnership encouraged foundations to expand its human resource and expertise in the field of higher education in Africa.

Knowledge was transferred in a significant way among the Partnership foundations. Most program officers interviewed acknowledged that they gain invaluable knowledge about which areas to fund, the institutions to support, and the experts to consult. For instance, Narciso Matos, Carnegie's former program director, commented, "I don't think any of our foundations would have had the knowledge that we were able to collectively acquire in that time simply by working together and having all of these meetings and workshops. I think that was a major advantage to all of us."[9] Knowledge transfer itself justified the amount of time and human resource invested by each foundation. As such, knowledge transfer was an important return on investment for members, adding value to the Partnership and providing critical information to the foundations. Finally, there was a connection between knowledge transfer and risk reduction. Investing in weak institutions represented an important risk for all philanthropic investors. Reducing this risk factor through collaboration was also an incentive for the Partnership's foundations. The Partnership was created to push the foundations to interact more frequently with each other, particularly with those foundations that were already actively involved in African higher education. The partnering foundations were dependent on each other to maximize their impact and maintain a high level of efficiency. The Partnership's complex organizational form preserved the individual choices and grantmaking strategies of each foundation, and accelerated knowledge transfer while reducing risks and increasing collaborative productivity.

The comparisons drawn between the foundations in the Partnership provide an insight into the role of US philanthropic foundations in higher education in Africa. These comparisons reveal the complexity of foundation collaborations and the mechanisms implemented by participants so that the Partnership could function smoothly. Institutional cultures of foundations influenced their strategic grantmaking and created a tension between the prerogatives of each institution and the needs of collective action. The dynamics of collaboration that operated in the PHEA served the foundations involved, despite an uneasy coexistence among each institution that stemmed from the desire to maintain their own specificities. However, Partnership foundations were able to find common ground and accomplish ambitious goals, despite the fact that they were founded in different socio-cultural eras and reflected interests and identities that grew out of various contexts.

Indeed, although the Partnership presented the seven foundations involved with an opportunity to maximize their grantmaking and deliver high-impact philanthropy in the field of higher education in Africa, their synergy was somewhat halted by the need to preserve the foundations' institutional culture. However, as a result of the collaborative work involving two or more foundations, some consensus was achieved after several successful initiatives. Moreover, the safeguarding of boundaries among the partners, which reflected the foundations' idiosyncratic individualism, led the foundations to surmount the Partnership's challenges by encouraging creativity and allowing for greater flexibility. Adapting the Partnership's format and operations to the needs of the foundations—rather than the other way around—generated more collaborative efficiency, particularly in the aggregation of reputation, knowledge transfer, and risk reduction. Indeed, the foundations rationalized a collaborative effort along a strategic alignment that fit their prerogatives. To a certain extent, this strategy offered some protection to the foundations against the possibility of failure and unproductive collaboration. The pressure for positive outcomes and accountability among Partnership members required the addition of better management processes. This pressure also highlighted the role of foundation managers in the normalization of these processes.

NOTES

1. September 26, 2011 interview in New York with Tade Akin Aina, program director, Carnegie Corporation of New York.
2. June 22, 2011 phone interview with Kole Shettima, program director, The John D. and Catherine T. MacArthur Foundation Nigeria office.
3. The Carnegie Corporation of New York Charter, Constitution and Bylaws (2011).
4. June 22, 2011 phone interview with John Butler-Adams, program officer at Ford Foundation's South Africa office.
5. June 22, 2011 phone interview with Kole Shettima, program director, The John D. and Catherine T. MacArthur Foundation Nigeria office.
6. July 12, 2011 phone interview with Raoul Davion, program officer, The John D. and Catherine T. MacArthur Foundation.
7. August 23, 2011 phone interview with Janice Petrovich, former program director at the Ford Foundation.
8. September 29, 2011 phone interview with David Court, former program officer at The Rockefeller Foundation.
9. September 9, 2011 phone interview with Narciso Matos, former program director, Carnegie Corporation of New York.

CHAPTER 5

When Foundations Work Together

Philanthropic partnerships between foundations are formed from time to time to tackle problems of scale related to specific issues such as serious diseases, environmental concerns, and poverty. These partnerships grow out of a mutual respect between foundations, the pairing of complementary strengths, and a collaborative process for planning and decision-making. Partnerships evolve through foundations' work on a shared set of goals and priorities in such areas as community and social development, environmental management, improvements in governance, health, education, and private sector development. Foundations can achieve greater impact when they join forces with other foundations. Wood and Gray (1991) define collaboration as a process that "occurs when a group of autonomous stakeholders of a problem domain engage in an interactive process, using shared rules, norms, and structures, to act or decide on issues related to that domain."[1] Collaboration implies sharing processes and mechanisms; it creates terrain for institutional interdependency, compelling partners to share authority and responsibility in order to fulfill their common mission. Although scholars such as Fleishman (2007) and Bacchetti (2006) argue that foundations are both wary of and selective about engaging in partnerships because of the additional costs and labor-intensive efforts that partnerships imply, including the risk of realizing more ambitious goals, foundations nonetheless seem to recognize the need to collaborate with others to surmount obstacles that they could not overcome alone.

Yet, there is a tension between the need for sustainable results and the push by foundations to generate high-impact solutions to big issues. In a famous essay on collaboration, Paul Brest, former president of The William and Flora Hewlett Foundation, wrote that foundations can work together to generate better ideas, build broader constituencies, and increase the amount of money available to achieve common goals. Reflecting on the motivations of funders, he also underlines the dangers that lie in working with others:

© The Editor(s) (if applicable) and The Author(s) 2016
F. Jaumont, *Unequal Partners*, Philanthropy and Education,
DOI 10.1057/978-1-137-59348-1_5

Some donors seem more interested in funding innovative programs with immediate visible impact than in achieving long-term, sustainable results. Some have low expectations of nonprofit organizations and treat an honorable mission as a substitute for impact. And doubtless some donors are motivated more by relationships and recognition than by achieving results. More fundamentally, personal philanthropy may sometimes be so profoundly emotional as to be invulnerable to rational analysis.[2]

As Brest indicates, the relationship between expectation and recognition is not always harmonious and often finds its disharmony at the human level. However, collaboration among foundations can develop the ability to serve mutually beneficial objectives and priorities.

The Partnership For Higher Education In Africa

The PHEA was a joint effort of the Carnegie Corporation of New York, Ford Foundation, John D. and Catherine T. MacArthur Foundation, The Rockefeller Foundation, The William and Flora Hewlett Foundation, The Andrew W. Mellon Foundation, and The Kresge Foundation to strengthen universities in Africa and support academic networks on the continent. Although the Partnership sought to impact the field of higher education across the African continent, actual funding was directed to higher education institutions in nine countries: Ghana, Kenya, Nigeria, Mozambique, South Africa, Tanzania, Uganda, Madagascar, and Egypt. The foundations also supported regional and sub-regional organizations and research consortia that furthered the development of higher education in Africa, such as the Nigeria ICT Forum of Partnership Institutions, the Regional Universities Forum for Capacity Building in Agriculture, and the African Population and Health Research Center, among many others. Overall, the PHEA contributed more than $450 million to build the core capacity of about 60 universities and support special initiatives proposed by research centers and academic networks across the continent. Each of the foundations had significant grantmaking programs in Africa prior to joining the Partnership. By joining forces, the foundations were able to broaden the scope of their impact, and in many ways, this strategy proved to be successful. The Partnership foundations had two clear collective goals. As clearly stated on the Partnership's website, the first was to advocate for the "indispensable contribution of higher education to social and economic development" in Africa. The second goal was to accelerate the "processes of comprehensive modernization and strengthening of universities in selected countries."[3] The scope of these goals, which none of the foundations could accomplish alone, necessitated an efficient inter-institutional collaboration. By characterizing African universities as engines of development, governance, and peace, the PHEA received the encouragement of leading figures such as the former Secretary General of the United Nations, Kofi Annan, who declared, "This is an outstanding display of global citizenship. We need to train teachers and build up research capacity; we need to strengthen open universities and distance learning programs; and we need to ensure that African institutions have access to the latest technologies." When the PHEA was launched, the challenges facing African universities included technical obstacles to participation in increasingly global intellectual communities, quality of African higher education institutions within international and local contexts, cost of and access to education, gender equity, and the position of higher education as a responsible partner in building democratic societies:

> Under the initiative, each foundation works with those institutions that fit its mission and priorities. Some grantees will serve as regional models of successful transformation and public engagement, and others will play a significant role in local development. The Partnership capitalizes on the distinctive contribution that each foundation can make through shared learning, and will enhance the ability of grantmakers to support sustainable improvements in university performance.[4]

In various statements, the Partnership foundations declared that their joint effort tested and demonstrated the best that philanthropy has to offer by pooling their knowledge, strategies, and resources. Together, they aimed to balance the academic with the practical, thus enabling universities to become more robust intellectual institutions that can effectively produce a new generation of scholars, analysts, scientists, technologists, teachers, public servants, and entrepreneurs to fuel African development. The core functions of the Partnership included providing financial support concentrated on universities in countries undergoing systemic public policy reform. The foundations sought to strengthen the ability of individual higher education institutions in their role as active participants within differentiated national systems of higher education, and encouraged inter-institutional collaboration.

The PHEA was, from the beginning, a presidential initiative. In 2000, the presidents of Carnegie Corporation of New York, The Rockefeller Foundation, John D. and Catherine T. MacArthur Foundation, Ford Foundation sought to make a public statement refuting the commonly accepted view that higher education was not a priority and that donors should focus on primary education (the opinion of the World Bank until recently). For the presidents, higher education went hand in hand with primary education.[5] In a press release, Vartan Gregorian, president of Carnegie Corporation, declared that: "The Partnership for Higher Education in Africa represents our commitment to Africa's next generation of leaders, who deserve an exemplary education to prepare them to help set the course for their nations' futures. We expect the universities in which we invest to become the foundation of a higher education network that will serve all of Africa for decades to come."[6] The initiative was launched in response to practical innovations implemented by many African universities. These institutions were breaking with outmoded traditions and embarking on major institutional and academic change, including new financial formulas, course structures, and governance practices. African governments were also increasingly recognizing the value of these reforms in national development and poverty alleviation. Commenting on the progress underway in many African universities, Judith Rodin, president of The Rockefeller Foundation, said, "Knowledge, innovation and talent are critical currencies needed to thrive in today's interconnected world, and Africa's universities are increasingly looked upon to generate the ideas and talent necessary to address Africa's challenges, on Africa's terms." Looking back on the Partnership's past accomplishments, Ford Foundation President Susan Berresford explained, "Our partnership began five years ago with the recognition that a quiet revolution was taking place in Africa making universities once again a source of innovation, training and scholarship. Such effort expands our commitment to the renaissance of African higher education and to its importance in Africa's future development." To this, Jonathan Fanton, president of the John D. and Catherine T. MacArthur Foundation added, "African universities that combine excellent, world-class education with programs of practical training are vital to progress, and it is heartening to see them emerge." The foundations identified an opportunity to generate significant impact in the field of higher education. Promoting change in universities encouraged the foundations to invest more funding in the initiative. By helping universities modernize, the foundations ensured that they could play a part in promoting processes of democratization, decentralization, and economic reform, thus extending the effect of their programs far beyond the field of higher education. The foundations sought to "reaffirm the importance of a vibrant intellectual environment in Africa in nourishing social, political, and economic transformation."[7] The Partners selected African universities and other academic networks in their efforts to stimulate "enlightened, equitable, knowledge-based national development." Together, these foundations formed a powerful and respected consortium that shared a common and ambitious objective.

In an attempt to define the Partnership's mission, the foundations established a set of goals and expectations that centered mostly on grant recipients and rarely on the foundations themselves:

> Selected universities and centers of intellectual inquiry will demonstrate ability to promote the free flow of ideas and enlarge the public sphere of their societies. They will exhibit a strong academic base as judged by international and local criteria, good governance, sound management, and through creative mixtures of public and private funding, financial stability. As part of the national higher education system, they will build and transfer a repertoire of skills essential for the development of their societies and the realization of individual and national aspirations. They will produce well-prepared high-level professional talent. They will reflect a quiet revolution in institution building in Africa that can unleash the talents of the continent for the well-being of its people and those beyond its borders.[8]

As such, the terms of the Partnership were set by its founders according to a vision shared by the four presidents of Carnegie Corporation of New York, Ford Foundation, The Rockefeller Foundation, John D. and Catherine T. MacArthur Foundation, and The Andrew W. Mellon Foundation, The William and Flora Hewlett Foundation, and The Kresge Foundation, who were invited to join a few years later, adhered to this vision.

Accountable to a wide range of stakeholders, foundations seeking to bring about sweeping reforms of public institutions must be able to deliver incremental results. Indeed, in most cases, a foundation must wait years before public policy results are evident, thus impact-seeking grantmakers must be willing to make a long-term commitment. The Partnership's 10-year commitment confirms this point. The Partnership's most significant accomplishment was to provide Internet bandwidth at affordable prices to African universities in desperate need of essential resources for research and teaching. Universities in several West African countries, utilizing Partnership funding, formed a consortium to purchase a sixfold increase in bandwidth in order to provide quality Internet service at a lower rate—a significant first step toward parity in the online world.[9] All participating foundations agreed on supporting the bandwidth initiative though not all foundations funded it.

Though all foundations committed to a large financial investment, each of them had a different approach to supporting higher education: Carnegie, for instance, was bound by its charter to fund commonwealth countries only, whereas John D. and Catherine T. MacArthur Foundation had a strong interest in human rights and pushed for the addition of Madagascar to the list of grantees. Additionally, Carnegie Corporation of New York had an interest in libraries that was not shared by the other foundations and Ford Foundation was already very active in Africa with four program officers on the continent before the Partnership even began.[10] In a famous essay on collaboration, Paul Brest warns:

> Foundations can work together to generate better ideas and build broader constituencies as well as increase the amount of money available to address common goals. However, collaboration has inevitable up-front costs in the time and effort spent in communicating and making decisions together with one's partners. The process can often be frustrating, and a beneficial outcome is hardly assured. At the end of the day, the extra effort is justified only if it has greater impact in improving people's lives.[11]

In a partnership, the process for approving projects can be quite challenging but immediate advantages include cutting costs and staff time, and multiplying the number of opportunities for funding. "Agreeing between foundations is the hardest thing to achieve," affirms Suzanne Grant Lewis, a PHEA coordinator, "on average, only two or three foundations will agree to fund the same project."[12] When the Partnership was formed, there was, as is often the case with new endeavors, some skepticism regarding the venture. As the foundations worked together and honed their relationship over the years, even the most cautious observers began to appreciate the benefits of collaboration. While African universities will ultimately determine whether the Partnership's efforts were successful, the words of Narciso Matos, Carnegie's program director and former secretary general of the Association of African Universities, underline the humility with which grantmakers should measure success in their funding effort:

We have learned to celebrate accomplishments by attributing success to the agency of the grantees rather than to the foundations. Visibility is essential for successful interventions to encourage other African governments, donors and investment agencies to support higher education and to reassure the foundations' trustees and leaders that money is being effectively invested. On the other hand, too much publicity might raise the expectations of other needy institutions and countries, leading policymakers to steer resources away from partnership universities toward other pressing needs not presently addressed by donors.[13]

The partnering foundations witnessed considerable progress within universities participating in the Partnership, in ways that bore directly on development and economic progress in their respective nations. In addition to the Internet Bandwidth initiative, the Partnership achieved many other significant victories. At South Africa's University of KwaZulu-Natal, the African Center for Crop Improvement established a 5-year PhD program to train plant breeders to develop new varieties of crops in hopes of bolstering the continent's home-grown food supply. Partnership support also led to the creation of the Journal of Higher Education in Africa—providing a forum for debate, critique, and analysis of issues facing African higher education. To catapult more women into leadership roles, over $10 million in academic scholarships was awarded to almost 1000 students attending universities in four African countries: Nigeria, South Africa, Tanzania, and Uganda. In Uganda, Makerere University worked with the government to implement hands-on programs to increase the quantity and quality of trained public servants, including a novel master's program in public health, aimed at supplying the country's districts with new health systems managers.

When the Partnership was launched, African higher education was at a crossroads after two decades of economic austerity and benign neglect. Recent attempts at the national and continental levels to re-energize and empower the continent coincided with the dawn of a new millennium. Although the issues to resolve were abundant, as the following statement by the Association of African Universities confirms, it was an opportune time for the foundations to reflect on new directions for policy and practice in African higher education:

Higher education in Africa has been characterized by high expectations and demand from key stakeholders, not matched by commensurate resource support; a small number of universities per country; low enrolment ratios at all levels, despite an enrolment explosion in the last 20 years that has stretched institutional facilities and capacities to breaking point; aging faculty, lack of incentives to attract younger staff and continued brain drain; weak private sector support and undeveloped culture of private contributions to universities; inadequate financial and logistical support from governments; weak linkage between academia and the social and productive sectors of the economy; and weak linkage with and provision of support to national and continental organizations.[14]

Though international donors' investment in higher education in Africa increased, collaboration among donors was still lacking in order to tackle issues of scale. However, meeting the development needs of the entire world is a complex and challenging task that no one institution can effectively address alone. Partnerships are essential to mobilize the world's technical and financial resources in support of development solutions. Even the World Bank acknowledged the need to foster collaboration between its departments and private funders, such as international foundations. To do so, the World Bank created a specific department supporting such collaborations in order to capitalize on the influx of cash and ideas generated by private foundations. Partnerships with foundations were important in order to:

> Gain knowledge and experience in good practice, research and information related to their specific country knowledge and sector expertise; share information in order to foster complementary work; deepen development work through consultation on corporate priorities such as country and regional assistance strategies, poverty reduction strategy papers, the Millennium Development Goals, and the Comprehensive Development Framework; consult on initiatives that are foundation based, yet complementary to Bank activities, such as research, pilots, evaluations, strategies, seminars and conferences; and enlarge Bank and foundation capacity to convene and support broad consortia of donors and specialists in regional or global initiatives through intellectual and financial support.[15]

As a contrast, several interviews with program officers highlighted a conscious effort on the part of foundations to distance themselves from the World Bank. Although the World Bank has welcomed collaboration with foundations in order to capitalize on the influx of cash and ideas generated by private philanthropy, partnering with the World Bank has not always been in the foundations' interest. Moreover, although the Partnership foundations were reluctant to collaborate with the World Bank, they still hoped to leverage funds from the Bank. The World Bank, along with other international donors, such as foreign development agencies, pan-African development funds, and American and European foundations, formed an interesting environment for foundations to maximize their investments.

Since foundations act as investors, the most fundamental form of collaboration is the aggregation of funds to produce results which any single funder could not accomplish.[16] Foundations can bring their knowledge and reputation as well as their funding to the table, as Paul Brest confirms in his essay on collaboration:

> Funders with common aims regularly share information in affinity groups—for example, Grantmakers in the Arts—as well as through informal exchanges. Hewlett Foundation staff meet annually with the presidents and program directors of peer foundations concerned with international family planning and reproductive health, and our Education Program routinely invites colleagues from other foundations to its annual meetings with grantees.[17]

The PHEA was founded on an affinity between the partnering foundations but sought to go beyond the mere exchange of information. Indeed, the

Partnership stemmed from the juxtaposition of seven foundations with distinct, even contrasting, institutional cultures, missions, strategies, and philosophies of development. These foundations coexisted and often funded similar universities in Africa but never coordinated their efforts. To echo Powell and DiMaggio (1991), institutions formed in different socio-cultural eras, such as the Partnership's foundations, coexist uneasily as they hold different interests and individualities and thus struggle to work collaboratively. Yet, the Partnership succeeded in pulling together some of the largest and most prestigious funders of the time to tackle issues in higher education development that not one foundation could have solved.

Every foundation has its own procedures, ranging from due diligence conduct, reporting expectations, monitoring, and evaluation to the particular forms and documents it has designed for those purposes. Collaborative grantmaking seeks to further the missions of both funders and their grantees. However, decision-making by consensus is not a highly efficient process; therefore participants in a partnership must learn how to make compromises. Moreover, there are risks involved for both grantors and grantees:

> Potential grantees may feel at greater risk when the identification of worthy organizations depends on the collective decision of a number of funders, which increases the chances of an all-or-nothing outcome. While this danger cannot be entirely discounted, funders are protective of their autonomy, and that they tend to exercise independent judgment on basic issues such as the selection of grantees.[18]

It is essential to understand how the dynamics of collaboration and interpersonal exchange contributed to producing a partnership of foundations which shared a single purpose. Foundations are all made of flesh and bone, served by program officers, directors, staff, vice-presidents and presidents, board members, and grantees with different takes on how philanthropy should impact a given field. Thus, emphasizing the human factor in the Partnership's activity offered the potential to examine the role of embedded institutional culture on the individuals who served the foundations. Indeed, foundations do have points of convergence, affinities, shared values, interests, and historical connections that can explain the inter-organizational dynamics that animated said foundations' collaboration. Collaborative action, in the case of the Partnership, did not occur in an institutional vacuum devoid of outside factors.

The interactions between the Partnership's actors and their beneficiaries offer an opportunity to examine the role of legitimacy-conferring processes. Ingram and Clay (2000) state that institutions affect not only strategies and interests but also patterns of relationships between actors, preferences, objectives, and identities. Multiple interactions occurred between the Partnership's foundation leaders, program officers, directors, and advisors. These actors assessed their participation in the Partnership, as well as the Partnership's strategy and potential impact, through the lens of their respective foundation's standards and processes. These procedures reflected socially acceptable and desirable norms and values among the Partnership's participants and grant recipients. They also provided justification and accountability for each actor's choices.

In a partnership, foundations can bring intellectual and reputational capital as well as financial capital to the table. However, since foundations are essentially investors, the most regular form of collaboration is the aggregation of funds between foundations, governmental institutions, or grassroots organizations. As such, between 2000 and 2010, the PHEA, which included seven foundations, provided $439.9 million in funding to higher education institutions in nine African countries. The processes of collaborative engagement and fund aggregation have the potential to generate greater impact and influence for foundations. Through the Partnership, these seven foundations became even more influential players in the field of African higher education. They not only increased their respective funding to African institutions but also formed a unified group of grantmakers whose collective power offered to change an entire field. By doing so, they drew attention as legitimate higher education developers and carried this legitimation power over to their beneficiaries. By promoting their collaborative engagement publicly and receiving media attention, the foundations highlighted a field worthy of investment. Recipients of their grants gained prestige and capitalized on this recognition to then attract more funds. Thus, understanding the Partnership's mechanisms helps understand how foundations rationalize their strategies and delineate their boundaries with other foundations in order to preserve their interests.

There are many types of partnerships and possibilities for collaborative engagement, spanning from a mere exchange of ideas and co-learning to more hybrid and organized structures such as strategic alignments, targeted collaborative funding, or the creation of a separate pooled fund. Collaborative grantmaking involves a number of labor-intensive activities, including due diligence, monitoring, and evaluation. Avoiding duplication of these efforts can save both the funders and grantees' time and money. From the funders' perspective, the greatest cost is the amount of time that collaboration can take. The time consumed is a function of the number of collaborating funders, the number of staff members tasked to the joint enterprise, the participants' willingness to compromise on matters of procedure and substance, and the internal structure and leadership of the group. The Partnership offered an interesting case of formal strategic alignment. The alignment allowed greater flexibility and control for the foundations while ensuring their full commitment. The Partnership was not a separate entity with its own charter, identity, pooled fund, or grantmaking programs. Initially, it was an informal relationship that grew out of discussions between the presidents of the four founding foundations and several senior staff. The Partnership eventually became a more elaborate structure which sought to go beyond the mere exchange of information and collaborative learning. It was formalized by an official agreement signed by the four foundation presidents. The following quote was excerpted from an interview with Raoul Davion, program officer at The John D. and Catherine T. MacArthur Foundation:

The design and structure [of the PHEA] was a semi-formal collaboration amongst the four foundations [Carnegie, Rockefeller, Ford, and MacArthur] where the initiative really grew out of discussions among the foundation presidents, the presidents of the four founding foundations and staff was then asked to operationalize this idea of working together in support of higher education. It grew out of shared recognition of commitment and interest in the field of higher education among the foundations. And, in that sense, it was launched before it was designed, in terms of how it actually operates.[19]

Aligning strategies and retaining separate grantmaking mechanisms seemed to offer fewer constraints than creating a pooled fund. The following quote, excerpted from an interview with Joyce Moock, former associate vice-president of the Rockefeller Foundation, offers an explanation as to why a separate entity could not have been created:

Now there have been partnerships on housing, transport, health issues, in which you simply go in and create a new entity, and everybody gives money to that entity, the entity has a secretariat, and it has whatever its own configuration is, and it forms a single funding pot. This couldn't happen in this field [of Higher Education in Africa], it was too close to the bone, and no foundation wanted to give up its interpersonal relationship with universities it has been working with for years and years, and have something bump up in between.[20]

A separate entity was seen as detrimental to the privileged relationship between foundations and grantees. Creating a separate fund would have forced foundations to relinquish control and power, reduced their individual visibility, and disrupted their other initiatives in Africa.

Introduced as an informal collaboration, the Partnership was actually formalized as a strategic alignment operation. This soon required even further formalization and organizational rationalization as the administrative burden of coordinating seven of the largest foundations in the USA grew. The strategic alignment initiated by the four founding partners—Carnegie Corporation of New York, The Rockefeller Foundation, Ford Foundation, and John D. and Catherine T. MacArthur Foundation in 2000—was later reinforced by The Andrew W. Mellon Foundation and The William and Flora Hewlett Foundation who joined in 2005, and by The Kresge Foundation in 2007. The partners also decided on a set of countries in which at least one foundation had previously worked that would become Partnership priorities for funding. With no other clear goals decided at the time of the launch, the functional mission was thus left in the hands of program directors and officers in each foundation. The Partnership was envisioned as an informal platform for information exchange among grantmakers. However, ambiguous decision-making and communication processes burdened the program officers and generated collaborative inefficiency. Because the Partnership had to be consultative, simple decisions were sometimes cumbersome. The program officers interviewed in this study stressed that there had not been a clear agreement vis-à-vis the objectives or main areas of focus of the Partnership. This initial lack of foresight and planning was a disadvantage in that the participants spent more time reaching decisions than necessary. While all participants understood that the Partnership was a presidential initiative, with naturally broad objectives, the lack of clear goals and measureable outcomes hampered the collaboration. More clarity and specificity would have helped the program officers involved determine what the Partnership was meant to accomplish. Yet, this lack of clarity is also revealing of the complexity inherent to the collaboration of several large foundations. Andrea Johnson, program officer at Carnegie Corporation of New York, articulates a similar view:

> It took forever to make decisions and negotiating when some, many if not most, of the partners would not be completely up front about what was behind their own decisions—not wanting to air their foundations internal politics in the discussion. So we would run into bottlenecks or outright walls without understanding why the wall was there or what was causing the bottleneck. We only knew that so and so was not agreeing to something, that everyone else was, or was hesitant or was throwing things back into the conversation that we thought had already been dealt with.[21]

Institutional constraints stalled the Partnership's decision-making processes and overall performance. This, in turn, impacted the potential for effective grantmaking which the foundations expected. Still, grantees in Africa understood these challenges and applauded the foundations' efforts to work together, as Njabulo Ndebele, vice-chancellor of the University of Cape Town, confirms:

> The foundations, although they have pooled this money into the Partnership for Higher Education in Africa, they still operate very much as individual foundations. I used to think that that was a problem, but looking back, I think that it was important for them to remain to follow their funding objectives. Now I know that what is lacking, what is missing, is not that the foundations chose to work differently within the Partnership for Higher Education in Africa framework, but where they sought to make an intervention, there wasn't a flexible policy environment for the foundations to plug in from the perspective of their own difference, but within the framework of the Partnership for Higher Education in Africa to achieve certain objectives.[22]

The Partnership's alignment model was the product of individual idiosyncrasies among philanthropic foundations which preferred to maintain a significant degree of independence by diminishing the collaboration's isomorphic processes. Nigerian sociologist Tade Akin Aina, program director at Carnegie Corporation of New York, offered the following interpretation:

> What the foundations did, you can call it confederation because it is not like partners in a legal practice, or a medical practice or a firm of architecture. Because there is a whole legal definition of partnerships, it exists as a norm. Partners can be dissolved, there is a right of veto, there is all of it. So, a confederation—and it was better than what I would have called a trust fund. A trust fund would have created a completely independent foundation or fund from the seven foundations. Because it will develop its own bureaucracy, it will have its own governing

structure, maybe its board of directors or will haggle at that level, it will have its own manager but then that really strains.[23]

This Partnership's equilibrium was better served as a confederation of foundations with equal rights, veto power, guaranteed seats, and no obligation to pool funds. The partnership was neither a legally binding arrangement that could dismiss partners through a vote, nor was it a separate entity with an independent governing structure. Thus, each foundation was able to retain a degree of power and independence. Individualistic interests were served while contributing and benefitting from the cumulative value of the Partnership.

COLLABORATIVE ENGAGEMENT AND INDIVIDUALISTIC INTERESTS

In terms of grants, there were two funding vehicles available to Partnership foundations: joint Partnership initiatives and individual foundation grantmaking. Through the organizational dynamics described in the previous section, this confederation-like structure resulted in a greater proportion of individual grants than joint grants during the 10-year collaboration. However, joint initiatives amounted to only 15 % of the overall partnership's grant total. The majority of grants were made by each individual foundation outside of the partnership. The PHEA was able to expand its resources by adding new foundations to the confederation. The average yearly disbursement from 2000 to 2004 was just over 30 million dollars; from 2005 onward, this value nearly doubled. This is a significant level of resource expansion. The total grand disbursement increased by over $135 million in the second phase. The resource expansion of the second phase can be explained by two factors: additional resources contributed by the founding members (the combined contributions of Carnegie Corporation of New York, Ford Foundation, The Rockefeller Foundation, and John D. and Catherine T. MacArthur Foundation increased by more than $45 million during this second phase), as well as new resources contributed by the added members (from 2005 to 2009, The Andrew W. Mellon Foundation, The William and Flora Hewlett Foundation, and The Kresge Foundation contributed over $90 million). Thus, two thirds of the Partnership's second phase resource expansion was due to the addition of new members. The founding foundations increased their involvement when other foundations joined (around 2005 for Mellon and Hewlett and 2007 for Kresge). Admitting new members did stimulate the expansion of resources and the amount of available funding, but it did not increase joint funding significantly. A 2004 evaluation highlighted this paradox and even questioned the validity of labeling certain joint grants as joint:

> These joint grants are actually individual grants as far as the grantees are concerned. The dividing line between joint and individual grants is not always clear— either to us or to the Partnership. There is evidence of considerable discussion

between the foundations and the Facilitator about whether certain grants are to be categorized as joint or individual.[24]

Because of the foundation's commitment to the Partnership over the years, longer-term planning and joint grantmaking was eventually achieved. The foundations exhibited a good understanding of the issues and challenges which plagued universities in several African nations. Although the PHEA excelled at information sharing, it fell short because of the refusal of the foundations to pool funds. Stuart J. Saunders, Mellon's senior advisor for the South Africa program, confirms this point:

> The advantages were to get a better understanding of what the other foundations were doing and what their approach was. Each foundation has a different way of doing its business and it did not affect our grant giving. We were giving grants in South Africa in the same way we would have done if there hadn't been a partnership. So, it did not influence our grant giving.[25]

By working together, the foundations expanded their monetary power to impact the field of higher education in Africa. Yet, they achieved this expansion by way of mostly separate individual investments, counted as Partnership investments, rather than joint funding around shared activities. For this reason, the line between joint and individual grants was blurred. Several evaluations pointed to this issue, acknowledging that there was evidence of extensive dialogue between the foundation officers and the Partnership coordinator about whether certain grants were to be categorized as individual or joint. In this vein, communicating about joint and individual achievements was even more complex, as the final Partnership accomplishments report demonstrates. Although the report captures key collective accomplishments in the first 10 pages, the remaining 80 pages provide a per foundation description of each partner's contributions. Communicating individual results thus served the goal of preserving the foundations' legitimacy in the face of a collaboration that did not yield significant joint results.

Differing objectives between foundations can be potentially circumvented but never resolved. This can be a healthy source of tension, driving each foundation to bring a different perspective to the table. However, if the partnership goals are not perceived as immediately relevant to a particular foundation's objectives, it makes it difficult to sustain organizational commitment. In the case of the PHEA, integration was avoided and joint programs were minimal; individual activities were assimilated and communicated as partnership activities. This was a logical adjustment; a strategic response to organizational and environmental rigidity; and a way to keep the Partnership afloat. Coordinating participants, delegating power, and clarifying decision-making processes were rendered difficult because of the fact that the participants were serving both the collaboration and an institution. Raoul Davion, program officer at the John D. and Catherine T. MacArthur Foundation, illustrated this point noting:

Ultimately, each person is a representative of an institution. The staff greatly enjoyed the opportunity to collaborate and learn from colleagues, but it did not change the reporting relationships and requirements that we each had internally. Thus, balancing the desire to take the ideas and move forward on a collaborative basis with the constraints imposed through the institutional structures that we each came from was a constant tension in the Partnership.[26]

Fortunately, the addition of a secretariat to facilitate operations eased this tension between collective efficiency and the foundations' individual strategies. Coordinating the Partnership via the secretariat became the favored mode of operation for all members. It clarified some of the intra-partner communications issues and provided better management methods of information exchange. Although the foundations all gravitated toward a tendency for individual action, they were able to establish significant homogeneity through the Partnership. Neil Grabois, former vice-president of Carnegie Corporation of New York, adds:

There is a natural tension in the foundations in part because they do very different things. Each one wants to be proud of a certain kind of accomplishment, and sometimes that pride can be swallowed in the sense that you can accomplish more if you do something together and then all take credit for it.[27]

Ownership, pride, and credit sharing did not always favor the Partnership; the limits of the Partnership lay, to some extent, in the individual culture of each participating foundation. In the words of David Court, a member of Kenya's Commission of Higher Education and a long-time East African representative of The Rockefeller Foundation, the issue of reaching coherence in the Partnership had a bearing on the overall structure of the collaboration:

The extent to which the individual partners were pursuing their own agendas, getting coherence proved to be a very tricky exercise. Partly, because of their historical focuses which differed and partly because you have individual perspectives on the part of the individuals involved, and even the countries in which they think the organizations should work in.[28]

The lack of coherence was attributed to the foundations' respective histories, focuses, and agendas. It was also linked to the varying perspectives brought by all participants, which ultimately complicated the collaboration. However, although the missions, preferences, and styles of the partner foundations differed widely, the consortium, despite its imperfections, was solidly grounded on the proximity of values and norms shared among the partner foundations. The value-added of working collaboratively was appreciated. Partnership participants unanimously acknowledged the immediate advantages of the Partnership, such as sharing information and goals, aligning strategies, and expanding the breadth of one's grant programs. This homogeneity enhanced the exchange of knowledge and information among the partners. Today, African universities are reemerging as critical engines for economic, social, and development progress in Africa. They have become a primary locus for innovation and are providing essential training for future African leaders in the public and private sectors.

NOTES

1. Wood and Gray (1991) p. 146.
2. Hewlett Foundation, Annual Report 2006, p. xv.
3. "About PHEA" Retrieved from the website of the PHEA on September 2010.
4. The Partnership for Higher Education in Africa, Core Statement. Retrieved from the website of the PHEA on September 2010.
5. The World Bank recognized later that an investment in primary education raises the grantees' GDP by 1.1 when an investment in tertiary education raises it by 5.5.
6. Retrieved from the website of the PHEA on September 2010.
7. Partnership for Higher Education in Africa, Press Release, 2000.
8. Partnership for Higher Education, Core Statement, What would success look like.
9. The bandwidth initiative initially allowed several universities to share 93,000 kilobits per second (kbps) of Internet bandwidth each month, paying an average cost of $2.33 per kbps per month. Most African universities currently pay an average of $7.30 per kbps per month. As recently as two years ago, the total bandwidth available to them was only 12,000 kbps. In Nigeria, the University of Ibadan has moved from having only 25 dial-up links to the Internet five years ago to a campus-wide system of 1000 networked computers using wired and wireless technologies. Sixty percent of all university operations are now online, up from zero in 2001.
10. In 2006, the Ford Foundation announced $75 million in new funding for its International Fellowship Program and $30 million to launch TrustAfrica, an Africa-based grantmaking foundation.
11. Brest (2006).
12. November 15, 2007 interview with Suzanne Grant Lewis, coordinator, PHEA.
13. Matos (2006), p. 5.
14. Association of African Universities, Strategic Plan 2003–2010 (2004).
15. Retrieved from the website of the World Bank on September 15, 2008.
16. Scale is a crucial determinant of success in the effort of a half-dozen foundations—Hewlett, Moore, Packard, Rockefeller Brothers, TOSA, and Wilburforce—to assist eight First Nations, the province of British Columbia, and the Canadian federal government in protecting 21 million acres of temperate rainforest on the central coast of British Columbia. (Cited in 2006 Paul Brest's essay on collaboration.)
17. Brest (2006).
18. Ibid.
19. July 12, 2011 phone interview with Raoul Davion, program officer at the MacArthur Foundation, Chicago.
20. June 24, 2011 interview with Joyce Moock, associate vice-president, The Rockefeller Foundation.

21. August 10, 2011 interview in New York with Andrea Johnson, program officer, Carnegie Corporation of New York.
22. Njabulo Ndebele, vice-chancellor, University of Cape Town, South Africa. Transcript Interview with Megan Lindow. 2009.
23. September 26, 2011 interview in New York with Tade Akin Aina, program director, Carnegie Corporation of New York.
24. Moja et al. (2004), p. 15.
25. June 22, 2011 phone interview with Stuart J. Saunders, senior advisor for South Africa, The Mellon Foundation.
26. July 12, 2011 interview with Raoul Davion, program officer at the MacArthur Foundation, Chicago.
27. August 19, 2011 interview with Neil Grabois, former vice-president of Carnegie Corporation of New York.
28. September 29, 2011 phone interview with David Court, former program officer at The Rockefeller Foundation.

BIBLIOGRAPHY

Bacchetti, Ray, and Ehrlich, Thomas. 2007. *Reconnecting Education and Foundations. Turning Good Intentions into Educational Capital.* Stanford: Carnegie Foundation for the Advancement of Teaching.

Brest, Paul. 2006. *On collaboration (or how many foundations does it take to change a light bulb?).* Menlo Park: Hewlett Foundation.

DiMaggio, Paul J. Powell, and Walter W. 1991. *The New Institutionalism in Organizational Analysis.* Chicago: University of Chicago Press.

Fleishman, Joel. 2007. *The foundation: A great American secret; How private wealth is changing the world.* New York: Public Affairs.

Gray, Barbara, and Wood, Donna J. 1991. Toward a Comprehensive Theory of Collaboration. *The Journal of Applied Behavioral Science,* 27(2): 139–162.

Ingram, Paul, and Karen Clay. 2000. The choice-within-constraints new institutionalism and implications for sociology. *Annual Review of Sociology,* 26: 525–546.

Matos, Marciso. 2006. The Partnership for Higher Education in Africa. *International Higher Education Quarterly,* 44: 5–6.

Moja T., J. Reddy, and A. White. (2004). *Evaluation of the Partnership for Higher Education in Africa.* Unpublished.

CHAPTER 6

The Authority of Foundation Presidents

Foundation presidents operate at a different level than their program directors, officers, advisors, or even governing boards. Although not typically involved in day-to-day operations, they play an important part in setting and attaining the foundation's goals. In this chapter, the influence of foundation leaders on the strategies and initiatives of the seven members of the PHEA is examined, as well as their relationships with their respective boards and their peers. Program officers, foundation experts, and university administrators were interviewed to develop a view from within that is rare in the literature on foundations. Foundation leaders, their board, and their staff have different, perhaps even opposite views on the role of the foundation, the needs of their beneficiaries, and on funding priorities. The PHEA served as a template for understanding how these foundations functioned. The Partnership was a complex machine to operate, according to a number of reports and testimonies. The coordination of Partnership activities required more reporting, more record-keeping, and more communication between the foundations' staff, the coordinating officers, the evaluators and consultants, the foundations' field offices, and the grantees. The Partnership's archives at Columbia University are rich with reports, memos, emails, and correspondences documenting its decade-long existence and provide a monumentally large dataset for gaining insight into the world of large US foundations. Foundations are made of flesh and bone, and the people behind them have fascinating stories to tell. However, before going any further, it is important to understand why the presidents of major US foundations were interested in forming a partnership dedicated to the development of universities in Africa.

© The Editor(s) (if applicable) and The Author(s) 2016
F. Jaumont, *Unequal Partners*, Philanthropy and Education,
DOI 10.1057/978-1-137-59348-1_6

LIKE-MINDED LEADERS

When the PHEA was launched, every sitting foundation president was a former university president. In fact, for most of the Partnership's existence, a majority of Partnership foundations were led by former university leaders:

As illustrated in Table 6.1, the leaders of most of the Partnership's foundations included six university presidents and two university deans. While the influence of foundations on higher education has been the subject of much discussion (Hollis 1938; Curli and Nash 1965; Bacchetti and Ehrlich 2007; Drezner 2011; Bernstein 2013), the Partnership foundations offer new insight on the revolving door between foundations and universities. Indeed, the presence of many former university leaders at the head of the foundations in the Partnership suggests that the American higher education system played an important role in shifting the foundations' focus toward higher education in Africa. As Hammack and Anheier (2010) observed, there has long been a close and symbiotic relationship between top foundations and major research universities. Through their connection to universities, foundations gain access to knowledge and cutting-edge research. They build links with networks of leading experts and scholars in areas which they want to change. Universities, on the other hand, gain access to funds to start new projects, develop existing initiatives, or build institutional capacity. Additionally, both foundations and universities benefit from an exchange in reputation and prestige, and at times an exchange in personnel, as foundation leaders and program directors are hired from within academic circles. In current philanthropic practice, universities constantly leverage funds from private and public donors. Leveraging funds from foundations presupposes that a university has established a healthy conversation with a foundation regarding possible areas of impact. The dialogue between foundations and universities in the USA has been steady and vigorous, and typically emphasizes the symbiosis between both parties which

Table 6.1 The PHEA's Foundation Presidents

President	Foundation	Presidency	Previous position
Jonathan F. Fanton	MacArthur	1999–2009	President, New School for Social Research
Gordon Conway	Rockefeller	1998–2005	Vice-Chancellor, University of Sussex
Vartan Gregorian	Carnegie	1997–	President, Brown University
Susan V. Berresford	Ford	1996–2007	Executive Vice-President, Ford Foundation
William G. Bowen	Mellon	1998–2006	President, Princeton University
Paul Brest	Hewlett	2000–2012	Dean, Stanford Law School
Judith Rodin	Rockefeller	2005–	President, University of Pennsylvania
Don M. Randel	Mellon	2006–2013	President, University of Chicago
Rip Rapson	Kresge	2006–	President, McKnight Foundation
Luis A. Ubiñas	Ford	2008–2013	McKinsey & Company
Robert L. Gallucci	MacArthur	2009–2014	Dean, Georgetown University

share more similarities than differences as Frederick Keppel, Carnegie's second president, noticed in 1930:

> It is an interesting coincidence that the aggregate endowment of our foundations and of our colleges and universities is approximately the same... The responsibilities of the trustees, both in the control of finances and in the general direction of activities, are the same. In both, important decisions are based on group rather than individual judgment and derive their significance from this fact. Almost without exception permanent foundation executives have had their training in universities... Furthermore, whenever a foundation needs temporary help, it turns uniformly to the university.[1]

The close relationship between foundations and universities described above suggests that both institutions have influenced one another for a long time. They have established positive processes of collaboration in support of high-impact change.

The idea behind the Partnership for Higher Education first emerged in a like-minded conversation between the presidents of Carnegie Corporation of New York and The Rockefeller Foundation. The Partnership was born out of personal relationships between foundation leaders who had in common the desire and the background necessary to orient their foundations toward the development of higher education. By working together, they hoped to leverage funds and compound their reputation and influence. This means that the foundation presidents were personally invested in the Partnership of Higher Education in Africa, at least in the beginning. Thus, the Partnership became a vehicle to promote their own interest in higher education through initiatives that the foundations would support jointly in order to reach the presidents' ambitious goals. Even though the Partnership foundations' endowments ranked among the top 50 in the USA, the presidents knew very well that they could not hope to solve an issue as sweeping as higher education in Africa alone. Consequently, presidents increasingly turned to inter-foundation partnerships and encouraged collaboration between the public and private sectors.

The Partnership for Higher Education was a unique endeavor in that it only included major independent foundations. Through this partnership, the presidents sought to demonstrate that universities in Africa could play a bigger role in the economic development of the continent: "Contrary to the wisdom that prevailed among funding organizations and governments, the foundations argued that Africa's future rests with the development of its intellectual capital through strong higher education systems, not just with the development of basic education."[2] With a shared interest and expertise in higher education, the founding presidents wanted to join forces to make the case for higher education on the African continent. The presidents channeled their vision for higher education in Africa through the program officers and program directors that represented their foundations at the Partnership's table. Directors and program officers were expected to run the day-to-day operations of the Partnership. As Janice Petrovich, former program director at Ford Foundation, said:

This was an initiative that was created among the presidents. The president of Carnegie took the lead in meeting with other presidents to help establish this collaborative. That first layer was the presidents. This made things a bit compli-cated because the presidents work at a very macro level and don't tend to give very detailed guidance to staff, so [we needed] to figure out what the presidents wanted. Staff had to go back and forth to their own presidents and then come together and try to figure out how to fit all these pieces together.[3]

The presidents instilled the Partnership with a high degree of priority and vis-ibility during its very early stages.

There is no clear power devolution in a foundation, some foundations hav-ing a more centralized power structure than others. Foundations diverge both in terms of their internal organization, decision-making procedures, and power sharing. At one foundation, for instance, an employee may be very autonomous at a relatively low level, while at another foundation, a relatively high-level staff member may not have much autonomy at all because of the nature of his or her foundation's internal organization. Consequently, decisions were not easily green-lighted by the Partnership's participants, or their hierarchies. This had a bearing on the overall efficiency of the Partnership, particularly when the foun-dations tried to leverage each other so as to generate high impact on higher education in Africa. The presidents' input added to the Partnership's complex power-sharing dimension, particularly with regard to developing a common strategy for the initial four, then seven, Partnership foundations. Each foun-dation president delegated power in his or her own way, leading to unequal levels of autonomy among program directors. At times, these differences made it difficult for foundation staff to work with each other, thus preventing the Partnership from fully delivering on its promises. Janice Petrovich confirmed this point:

> The difficult role that the people who sat around the table had is that they were able to discuss ideas but often were not able to come to a decision at the table because they needed to go back to their foundations and check. And that was because they were representing the presidents and they needed to make sure the president was okay with everything that was happening. So they would go back and report. And it took a long time for any kind of joint product to emerge, because the presidents had to be on board.[4]

The strict chain of command described above, coupled with the relative indeci-sion of the actors involved, highlights a tense relationship between the presi-dents who did not delegate effectively to their program officers and the officers who needed to be entrusted with more authority. This situation was com-mented upon by several program officers, including Raoul Davion, program officer at The John D. and Catherine T. MacArthur Foundation:

> The leadership wanted to remain active and remained active in the partnership's operations and that was really an asset in terms of having the support and the

commitment of the foundation presidents. But, also I think it encumbered somewhat the decision making processes that the partnership utilized.[5]

The Partnership's program officers had to gain the support of their presidents
and work around the interferences and inefficiencies that are the inevitable
byproduct of such a large collaboration.

THE PRESIDENTS AND THEIR BOARDS

Foundation leaders and their boards often coexist with views, interests, and even
identities that grew out of different contexts. Boards of trustees may include
members of the founder's family (as is the case with The William and Flora
Hewlett Foundation and The Rockefeller Foundation), or university presidents
(as is the case at Carnegie Corporation of New York with the presidents of
the University of Baltimore, Georgetown University, or the University of Saint
Andrews). It is not unusual that a foundation board member, or even a senior
staff, sits on another foundation's board (as was recently the case with Ford's
president who was a trustee of the Kresge Foundation, or Ford's director of
democratic participation and governance, who sat on the board of the Hewlett
Foundation). Boards also include experts in a given field, artists, scientists, and
legal counselors. And in most cases, boards include corporate executives. The
board's decisions can have a bearing on the foundation's organizational structure and decision-making process. The board not only offers stewardship on
financial and human resources matters but also sets the foundation's grantmaking and programmatic strategies. Finally, the board hires the foundation's
chief executive. In many cases, board members come from the corporate world.
Whereas the foundation presidents' backgrounds have usually been the humanities or social sciences, with a few notable exceptions such as Ford Foundation's
previous president, Luis Ubiñas, who spent 18 years at McKinsey & Company
where he worked with telecommunications, technology, and media companies.
During his 5-years at Ford, he tried to change the foundation's institutional
culture by conducting a large internal restructuring that reduced drastically
the number of initiatives supported by Ford. This, in turn, was problematic for
presidents who had to justify the validity of partnering with other foundations
to their board. Several meetings among foundation presidents debated upon the
importance of leveraging funds as a key goal of the Partnership, and whether
the Partnership had been successful in accomplishing that goal. Several foundation boards (The Rockefeller Foundation in particular) made it difficult for
presidents if this goal was not clearly attained. Additionally, the boards expected
high impact similar to what the Partnership was able to accomplish with the
Bandwidth Consortium. The collective weight of the foundations allowed the
Partnership to significantly improve Internet bandwidth and technical expertise
for many universities. In the early twenty-first century, lowering the cost of
bandwidth in Africa was very important because the universities were not well
connected. This issue stopped them from being a part of the global community
and even internally within the country to operate and have access to literature,

research articles, or anything else. The cost of bandwidth and the lack of techni-cal support were recognized early on as primary obstacles by the foundations, an issue which they were able to solve thanks to their joint efforts.

Perhaps as a consequence of this relative tension between foundations and their governing bodies, certain initiatives were given preference over oth-ers. For instance, the presidents wanted to put more emphasis on economies of scale which transpired from a new penchant toward a market-based and technology-based approach to achieving high impact. For some foundations, this focus came directly from their boards which were often composed of economists (as was the case with the John D. and Catherine T. MacArthur Foundation), or business leaders (as was the case with most of the foundations' boards). The Partnership was seen as a way to leverage more funds and accom-plish goals that a foundation could not accomplish alone, thus generating a more significant impact. The decision to move away from a traditional grant-making strategy and to include clear and measurable indicators of impact was made with the promise to attain major breakthroughs quickly. In this light, it is hardly surprising that the Partnership's foundation embarked wholeheartedly upon endeavors outside of their comfort zone, notably in the field of ICT in Africa. The presidents were keen on a project that sought to expand Internet bandwidth for African universities. It was clearly a concern of interests to the presidents and as such it became a key initiative which drove all Partnership participants into forming the Internet Bandwidth Consortium which became the Partnership's signature initiative. On the other hand, when a topic received unenthusiastic responses from the presidents or their boards, it would soon be dropped or revised extensively, as was the case with an initiative called the Higher Education Advocacy and Research Network which originally sought to support and strengthen education schools and African higher education as a field of studies. Not all of the presidents considered the field of developing education schools a priority. Perhaps the sector did not carry enough market-based importance, or the promise of delivering the sought-after quantifiable results.

At the beginning of the twenty-first century, many international foundations—through their boards, their leaders, and their staff—were actively re-evaluating the purpose and relevance of their foundations' mission, and the place they collec-tively occupied in the conversation on issues that mattered for the world they lived in. In these early years, the foundations' preference for market-based and technol-ogy-based strategies, combined with measurable indicators of success, highlighted a paradigm shift than had taken the world of foundations by storm. The more traditional approaches of foundations were often criticized for lacking tangible results. And the foundations involved in the PHEA were not immune from this paradigm shift. Their vision for higher education in Africa reflected this change, and diverging views on what the future of African higher education should look like would clash around the Partnership's table. The Partnership's stated goal was to help universities become "engines of development" on the African continent. Historically, the universities' primary role, at least in Anglophone Africa, was to train civil servants. Making the case for higher education development on economic rather than cultural grounds implied that universities should train people for jobs in industry, rather than create an enlightened, educated citizenry as their primary function. This placed the foundation presidents in an ambivalent situation, considering their own background in the humanities and the new directions which their boards favored. This was commented upon by Phillip Griffiths, an advisor for The Andrew W. Mellon Foundation:

> There was not among the foundation presidents, a hands-on understanding, in my experience. They thought that the case for universities should be made on cultural grounds more than economic grounds.[6]

This point of view on the role of foundations and that of their presidents' is worth exploring. The uneasiness of the boards with regard to what a university or a foundation should do grew out of the convergence of academic institutions toward distinct, even opposite, patterns of reproduction and development as those of the corporate world. Large foundations, like large universities, have resisted pressures toward these business-oriented ideals, and continue to avoid these new standards by conducting their work unfettered. The tension between preserving this difference and aligning to a market-based approach had a bearing on both the Partnership's results and the results of each individual foundation.

On Leadership and Ownership

Although the Partnership presented the seven foundations with an opportunity to have greater impact on the field of higher education in Africa, their synergy did not succeed in delivering the full potential of the Partnership's promise. Instead, several institutional challenges plagued the Partnership. These included unclear objectives, technical obstacles to achieve joint funding, and the failure to expand the Partnership's resources. There was limited consensus and a low probability of collaboration, as there were few initiatives that involved more than two or three foundations. Moreover, a typical foundation grant is three years, once renewable, and most foundation bylaws dictate the duration of a grant. Six years is the maximum time for a particular project to be supported by a foundation. This obviously raises issues of financial sustainability for the initiatives supported by foundations, and underlines a degree of urgency under which foundation leaders have to work, and their need for short-term results when considering their boards' expectations. Nevertheless, the Partnership foundations set out to make the case to governments and international donors that the universities could be engines of economic growth in Africa, not just institutions that trained civil servants. This is a notion that is still not well understood by African governments, nor even within the African university community. To get government support, however, universities would need to train sufficient numbers of scientists or engineers in areas of science and engineering that are directly relevant to economic growth. That connection between university community and the emerging private sector in Africa was almost nonexistent.

Through their position of authority and their interest or disinterest in certain issues, the presidents played an important part in setting their foundations' agendas. Consequently, petitioning episodes occurred frequently between program officers. This divergence of perspectives between foundation leaders and program officers is common, and reflects a healthy interaction that triggers some internal diplomacy and subtle maneuvering. For instance, the Partnership was so time consuming to administer that it needed a central coordination unit with additional staff so as to remove some of the Partnership's administrative burden from the program officers' already-demanding responsibilities. But the presidents were not interested in adding staff or creating a centralized decision-making body that would oversee the foundations' activities. They feared that this would result in creating a bureaucracy, and preferred to leave the Partnership in the hands of their program officers so as to preserve each foundation's autonomy. It took a joint recommendation of staff to change their views. Andrea Johnson, a program officer in Carnegie's higher education in Africa office offered the following comment:

> The reason that we didn't have an office of secretariat was because the presidents didn't want it. They saw it as less operational and more as a learning group. The staff envisioned it as more operational—identify things to fund together, either jointly funded or aligned funding but heading in the same direction. That immediately ran into problems.[7]

Agreement among program officers became a prerequisite for responding to the presidents' criticism and divergent views. In the case of the coordination unit, the program officers were successful in making collective decisions and recommendations that would be accepted by their presidents. The presidents of the foundations would meet once a year and this was the only time that they were collectively focused on the PHEA. The secretariat and officers would have time to present, and would receive a collective communication from the presidents explaining how they wanted the program officers to proceed. But a lack of clarity in the president's directions impaired the effectiveness of the executive committee, and in fact the Partnership as a whole, which would have benefited from a much greater involvement of the foundation presidents. Not all of the presidents were aware of what the Partnership was doing. Foundations run many different programs and after the initial commitment, the presidents went on to other projects and did not care to stay involved in the Partnership's day-to-day affairs. There were some exceptions. The most active foundation presidents were Vartan Gregorian from Carnegie Corporation of New York and Jonathan Fanton from John D. and Catherine T. MacArthur Foundation. They gave much clearer direction to their staff than the other foundation leaders did. However, for a majority of interviewees, more personal involvement from the presidents, and more involvement from their board, would have generated more efficiency in the Partnership.

Foundations change significantly when there is a change in their leadership. New presidents bring along a shift in priorities which might reflect their board's new objectives, or simply an adjustment to an internal or external factor—that is, a crisis such as the 2008 economic downturn which took a toll on the foundations' endowments. The issue of president turnover is a constant theme. The decision to terminate the Partnership became a reality when the boards of Ford Foundation and The Rockefeller Foundation changed their presidents. David Court, a former program officer for The Rockefeller Foundation commented:

> Foundations change when they get new presidents who want to create something totally different in structure and in focus. But, neither Ford nor Rockefeller changed their Presidents until towards the end of the period in question. It was towards the end of the second phase that Rockefeller and Ford changed, and that created an impossible situation for the Partnership.[8]

In this particular case, leadership and ownership are clearly connected, and the change of leadership which occurred toward the end of the Partnership triggered its termination. Indeed, the leadership change at Ford and Rockefeller sounded the end of the Partnership. Andrea Johnson commented:

> The presidents turning over ultimately led to the demise of the partnership because they just did not have the commitment. Some were just not interested in higher education, for others it wasn't theirs. There was a real ownership question.[9]

This comment and the idea of presidential "ownership" of the issue of higher education raise a serious question. To a large extent, the founding Presidents owned the issues undertaken by the Partnership of Higher Education in Africa such as strengthening the capacity of universities in Africa, helping them transform into engines of development for the continent, creating the next generation of Faculty, or providing greater access for women in graduate programs. The Partnership founders created awareness on these issues by putting on them a microscope for their entire organization, and other foundations, to focus on solving them. These issues reflected on them, and as leaders owning those issues they were able to lead by example. Without ownership, there can be no leadership. The Presidents' turnover takes on a different meaning when it is placed in the larger leadership-versus-ownership discussion. Dina El'Khawaga, former program officer at Ford Foundation's office in Egypt, comments:

> Leadership change is the most critical challenge. But it is important that in the meantime over 2000 to 2010 many foundations have seen their leadership changing. We got a new president at Ford. At Rockefeller, they got a new president. At MacArthur, they left, dealing with an incoming new president. So, every single foundation president came and revisited the whole thing to make his or her own footprint. And it was challenging.[10]

As a consequence, the presidents of the Partnership's foundations decided to close the Partnership secretariat and not embark on a third formal phase with a public pledge of funding. At first, they planned on closing it in just two months. Senior participants persuaded the presidents to continue the Partnership until the planned end in 2010. In theory, the work would continue among the foundations but without a coordinating body. In practical terms, that was difficult to carry out, especially as new priorities emerged for foundations. But the general feeling among program officers was that they would have liked to have participated in the Partnership for a longer period, because toward the end of the Partnership, they were becoming more effective as a group. More funds were invested and counted as joint investments toward the end of the Partnership. In actuality, terminating the Partnership put program officers in an awkward position vis-à-vis their grantees. Justifying the decision to end ten years of collaboration, the impact of which is hardly measurable in the short term, undermined their position with partners on the ground and the sustainability of various projects. With new presidents at several foundations, it may have made sense to end the collaborative. However, some participants felt that there could have been more thoughtful planning on how to sustain or continue the work begun by the Partnership. As described in a final report, the decision to terminate the Partnership left the program officers "scrambling to explain the implications of the decision with their grantee organizations including how those organizations could sustain the work."[11] The difference in perspective translated into systematic negotiations between different hierarchical levels. These negotiations, which played a role in influencing the orientations and good functioning of the Partnership in general, were first meant to reconcile the differences in perspectives between foundation presidents and their staff. The presidents were the ultimate bearers of legitimacy and accountability in the foundations which composed the Partnership. Balancing the reality of joint grantmaking and collective decision-making with their validation and expectations was a common dilemma for the Partnership's program officers and directors who strove to defend their point of view as well as that of their grantees. Arguably, the authority of foundation leaders had an impact on the independence of Partnership foundations and their ability (or inability) to collaborate, particularly as the Partnership was initiated by the presidents themselves in order to deliver a strong message regarding the importance of higher education in Africa.

NOTES

1. Keppel (1930), pp. 10–11.
2. Grant et al. (2010), p. 5.
3. August 23, 2011 phone interview with Janice Petrovich, former program director for the Ford Foundation.
4. August 23, 2011 phone interview with Janice Petrovich, former program director for the Ford Foundation.

5. July 12, 2011 phone interview with Raoul Davion, program officer at the MacArthur Foundation, Chicago.
6. July 20, 2011 phone interview with Phillip Griffiths, advisor for The Andrew W. Mellon Foundation.
7. Parker (2010), p. 32.
8. September 29, 2011 phone interview with David Court, former program officer for The Rockefeller Foundation.
9. August 10, 2011 interview in New York with Andrea Johnson, program officer for the Carnegie Corporation of New York, USA.
10. August 16, 2011 phone interview with Dina El'Khawaga, former program officer for the Ford Foundation's office in Egypt.
11. Parker (2010), p. 35.

BIBLIOGRAPHY

Bacchetti, Ray, and Thomas Ehrlich. 2007. *Reconnecting education and foundations. Turning good intentions into educational capital.* Stanford: Carnegie Foundation for the Advancement of Teaching.

Bernstein, Alison R. 2013. *Funding the future: Philanthropy's influence on American higher education.* Lanham: Rowman and Littlefield.

Curti, Merle, and Roderick Nash. 1965. *Philanthropy in the shaping of American higher education.* New Brunswick: Rutgers University Press.

Drezner, Noah D. 2011. *Philanthropy and fundraising in American higher education. ASHE higher education report.* San Francisco: Jossey-Bass.

Grant Lewis, Suzanne, Jonathan Friedman, and John Schoneboom. 2010. *Accomplishments of the Partnership for Higher Education in Africa, 2000–2010.* Rep. New York: New York University.

Hammack, David C., and Helmut K. Anheier (eds.). 2010. *American foundations. Roles and contributions.* Washington, DC: Brookings Institution Press.

Hollis, Ernerst V. 1938. *Philanthropic foundations and higher education.* New York: Columbia University Press.

Keppel, Frederick P. 1930. *The foundation. Its place in American life.* New York: The MacMillan Company.

Parker, Susan. 2010. *Lessons from a ten-year funder collaborative. A case study of the Partnership for Higher Education in Africa.* Clear Thinking Communications. St. Johnsbury, VT

PART III

Foundations & the Question of Legitimacy

CHAPTER 7

The Legitimacy of American Foundations

In his foreword to Hammack and Heydemann's *Globalization, Philanthropy and Civil Society* (2009) Kenneth Prewitt called for more theoretical inquiry in the study of grantmaking foundations, particularly from the institutionalists among social scientists. Organized philanthropy, he states, "is not only in and of the civil society sector; it has a vital interest in expanding that sector. This is where philanthropy finds the institutions which, for their part, legitimate philanthropy by carrying out philanthropic missions" (p. viii). Thus, to gain or maintain legitimacy in this field, foundations rely on their grant recipients and other institutions which grant them legitimacy and ensure the continuation of their work. Foundations depend on their grantees to both absorb obligatory spend-out funds and fulfill their mission to serve the public good. Successful philanthropic action is impossible without an awareness of the institutional principles outlined above, which are often projected through foundations' work abroad. What follows is a narrative arc from goal-making, to strategic collaboration, to legitimacy maximization, all with an emphasis on two concepts: collaboration and legitimacy. While the Partnership's stated objective was to aid African universities, the foundations also paid close attention to their grantees, while building an agenda that suited their individual mission. The data included interviews with individuals directly involved in the Partnership and who received grants from one or several foundations. The discussion presented below illustrates how a group of respectable foundations orchestrated processes of legitimation to substantiate individual and collaborative choices and to promote their international philanthropy. As a result, there were multiple relationships that informed the given foundations' engagement with the partnership: the relationship on the ground between the foundation and a given university, the rapport among the various foundations both on the ground and in the USA; and the relationship between the foundation officers and their grantees. As such this chapter gauges the types of relationships that determine the notion of partnership. It traces the contours and identifies the

© The Editor(s) (if applicable) and The Author(s) 2016
F. Jaumont, *Unequal Partners*, Philanthropy and Education,
DOI 10.1057/978-1-137-59348-1_7

various institutional factors that limit equal participation between funders and beneficiaries, and thus questions the legitimacy of foundations within the context of an asymmetry of power. Following Aldrich and Fiol (1994), legitimacy is assessed in this chapter in terms of the foundations' ability to serve the needs and interests of universities and higher education organizations. Most directly, legitimacy emerges as a form of exchange between foundations and universities. These organizations do not exist in a vacuum, and must conform to the external pressures of cultural norms and values in addition to the internal rules and expectations that govern their institutional behavior. Foundations produce outputs—funds, recognition, prestige, and advocacy—that universities value and, in return, volunteer their support. Therefore, the environmental constraints that determine an organization's structure and practices are examined, and also particular attention is paid to issues of power, interests, and the potential for organizational legitimation. This institutionally focused framework can potentially offer a clearer view of foundations and their environment, as well as the processes of legitimation that guide their behavior. The foundations examined in this chapter are entities that were established under private auspices and that are privately governed, and which use the income generated by their endowment or their endowment itself to support various educational, cultural, scientific, and other charitable objectives.

Environmental constraints on behavior are often considered to be undesirable, as they are thought to restrict creativity and limit an institution's ability to adapt. Recent studies discuss the activities of US foundations abroad in relation to environmental forces (Kiger 2000, 2008; Sanborn and Portocarrero 2005; Karoff 2008; Friedman and McGarvie 2003). Kiger (2008) provides a historical account of US foundations' international work while assessing the impact of globalization on foundations and philanthropists. However, his conclusions only briefly address the absence of environmental restriction on the foundations' actions, which greatly benefitted their operations and reputation. Lester Salamon (in Hewa and Stapleton 2005) highlights that foundations and civil society in general are "both a consequence and a cause of globalization. More precisely, many of the forces driving the contemporary process of globalization are also contributing to the growth of the civil society sector internationally."[1] Peter Frumkin (in Hewa and Stapleton 2005) summarizes the limited extent of overseas funding by American foundations (less than 12 % of grant dollars during 1990–1998). He stresses that international grants addressing issues such as socio-political change, innovation, redistribution, and pluralism are likely to involve funders in a way that is notably different from their domestic counterparts. He concludes that "the most important thing for international grantmakers to remember is that the potential for major and sudden impact increases as one moves up from micro to macro levels—from individual to organizational to network to policy levels."[2] Foundations improve their reputations through effective grantmaking, which contributes to their perceived accountability. In this manner, a foundation's reputation enhances its strategy with more room to maneuver. Deephouse and Carter (2005) demonstrate that legitimacy and reputation have a close connection and are equally influenced by environmental and institutional forces. They also stress that an organization with a strong reputation is able to deviate from standard practices and still maintain status and legitimacy. Prewitt (in Prewitt et al. 2006) argues that foundations should be analyzed for what they have "effectively achieved rather than what they have been unable to accomplish."[3] Most researchers do not account for the internal and environmental dynamics that influence foundations. They also fail to emphasize that performance and accountability are essential for a grantor's reputation and legitimacy.

Foundations can also leverage reputation and legitimacy through strategic partnerships, particularly when foundations take on high-impact missions. Brinkerhoff (2005) highlights several strategic options for reputation enhancement which directly lead to legitimacy. These options include partnering with other foundations that already possess the desired forms of legitimacy or maximizing reputation within the foundation. A partnership of foundations with comparable reputations has the potential to maximize each partner's reputation and improves other organizational elements such as legitimacy. This underscores the need for a more institutionally focused approach to the study of foundations, one that simultaneously assesses and compares factors motivating foundations whether they are institutional, environmental, or actor-based. Foundation officers with specific capabilities, perceptions, and preferences interact according to different patterns, or modes, depending on their foundations' legitimation mechanisms. These patterns can also be observed among officers working in international organizations (Atlani-Duault 2009, 2011). Diana Leat (in Amheier 1999), for instance, examined the organization and management of British foundations and their grantmaking behavior. She interviewed staff in a representative sample of 30 fundraising and endowed foundations in Great Britain that were primarily concerned with issues of social welfare. After describing different styles of grantmaking, Leat argued that foundations work under a number of unique constraints. For instance, if there is an endowment, foundations are legally bound to respect the wishes of the donor. While this sounds straightforward, the initial donor's wishes are often broad (e.g., promote the well-being of humanity; diffuse knowledge) and therefore difficult to fulfill. Carnegie Corporation of New York mission is to "promote the advancement and diffusion of knowledge and understanding," but this ordinance is vague enough to be adapted and interpreted to suit the foundation's immediate objectives, which may be redefined at will. Moreover, trustees who have the responsibility of carrying out the donor's wishes often have interests that diverge from the donor's, and because trustees are not accountable to any one person, the organization can easily drift away from its original mission.

Because of external constraints on revenue and the need to remain autonomous, organizations possess both the desire and the ability to negotiate their position within those constraints using a variety of tactics, such as co-opting sources of constraint for more autonomy in order to pursue organizational interests. A discussion of this type of behavior is therefore central to understanding an institution. Fleishman (2007) asserts that most large foundations that are serious about their grantmaking fields already focus on strategies aimed at building on prior experiences in the same field. Foundations bypass institutional and environmental constraints by choosing to maximize their resources within a single field. They prioritize accumulating knowledge as they go forward. However, they often fail to share this knowledge with the outside world. These strategies take into account the pressure of environments and institutions with which foundations interact. Bacchetti and Ehrlich (2007) suggest that, in shaping strategies for education grants, foundations should make the building of "educational capital" their goal—that is, the generation and accumulation of knowledge toward the best solutions for the problems at hand. Moreover, the authors strongly urge that such strategies be developed jointly by individual foundations in partnership or in collaboration with other foundations and with groups of beneficiary educational institutions. Bacchetti and Ehrlich make a persuasive case that, in order to do so, foundations must first become "relentless learning organizations" by continuously studying their own impact and the processes that produce it. Moreover, they correctly point out that foundations cannot become "learning organizations" without becoming more public, visible, and transparent about their work, without subjecting their efforts to critical review and discussion, or without building on their own and on others' learning to guide future practice in the field. Both the dialogue with beneficiaries and the learning process that is entailed not only increase transparency but also can increase a foundation's legitimacy, as the following sections demonstrate.

Skepticism About the Role of Foundations

Several researchers have described the accomplishments of US foundations with skepticism, from the professionalization of public health to strengthening the non-governmental organization sector and research institutions (Clotfelter and Ehrlich 1999; Nielsen 2004). There is often uncertainty surrounding the legitimacy of philanthropy, particularly when it is strategically oriented toward high-impact endeavors. As Claire Gaudiani (2003) writes:

> Donations become dangerous when they encourage dependence or entitlement, when they engender deep bitterness, or when the donor's courage or good judgment fails and politics and ideology are permitted to transform the gift into an embarrassment or a burden. Some donations are destructive because of the causes they fund, campaigns against the very democracy and equality that we need to balance capitalism.[4]

Many acts of charitable giving fail in their stated goals and some are actually harmful, as foundation critics have pointed out over and over (Wormser 1958). In a 2014 article in *The Atlantic*, Gara Lamarche, former president of Atlantic Philanthropies, declares that "the leadership of American philanthropy jeopardized health-care reform in order to let the rich shield their money from taxation." He concludes that philanthropy is not only undemocratic in the way all decisions are made based on the donor's will—or at times mood—but also "quite capable of acting like agribusiness, oil, banks, or any other special-interest pleader when it thinks its interests are jeopardized." Yet, unlike a business, foundations do not have products, services, customers, authorities, or even competitors to be accountable to (Gaudiani 2003). However, foundations, like businesses, require legitimacy to attract constituents' support and continue to exist. The legitimacy of foundations is still intensely debated, particularly with regard to higher education and international development. Recent studies on foundations and higher education analyze whether foundations have become patron or bully in their recent relationship with universities. For instance, Baccheti and Ehrlich (2007) argue that in order to build educational, social, or cultural capital, foundations tend to "reinvent the wheel" and hardly adapt to local conditions and customs. Although these authors do not discuss directly the importance of legitimation in the foundations' operations, they do highlight the importance of local environments as a source of public recognition and acceptance. But, more importantly, the extensive literature on philanthropic foundations has questioned and continues to question the legitimacy of foundations, particularly when grants are used to transform institutions or entire fields.

The literature on philanthropic foundations also questions the aspirations of international foundations, particularly US foundations involved in capacity development in developing countries. At times, foundations are found to be working both with and against US foreign policy, seizing opportunities to operate internationally. For instance, The Rockefeller Foundation awarded grants for sending medical literature and small items of equipment to Soviet institutions in the 1920s (Rosenbaum 1989). Similarly, during the Cold War, Ford Foundation put into operation a non-governmental cultural diplomacy program to offset Communism (Dedrick 1997; Dowie 2002). The USA's influence abroad developed between the 1890s and the interwar period, revealing its full force after 1945. This influence helped to spread Western medicine around the world, including the establishment of medical schools in China (Bullock 1973), thus promoting international relations. Increasingly, during that time, foundations took a more active role to initiate change in society (Hewa and Stapleton 2005). For instance, Ford Foundation funding of intercultural publications, with a publishing house established in 52 countries, was the first major effort demonstrating a determination to play a role in international relations (Gregory 2000; Tournès 2002).

Questions regarding ideology, coercion, and foundation activity have been debated repeatedly by scholars many of whom often pinpoint foundations' problematic fostering of pro-US values and reinforcement of the US hegemonic construction over developed or developing nations. Joan Roelofs (2003) concludes that foundations are prime constructors of hegemony because they promote consent and discourage dissent against capitalist democracy. This obscures the frontiers of power and influence; instead it supplants democratic institutions with a "new feudalism." This belief echoes earlier studies which often considered foundations as relatively unfettered and unaccountable concentrations of wealth and power. Foundations were perceived as entities able to buy intellectual capital, advance causes, and delineate a society's focus (Whitaker 1974b; Arnove 1980). Darknell (in Arnove 1980) even argues that Carnergie Corporation of New York programs in higher education have been consistent with the interests of US corporations.

Other studies on US foundations question, through the lens of cultural hegemony, the benefits and drawbacks of foundation work (Berman 1971; Whitaker 1974; Arnove 1980; Brison 2005). These views often conclude that older foundations such as Carnegie Corporation of New York, The Rockefeller Foundation, and Ford Foundation have been accused of having a corrosive influence on society. Arnove (1980) depicts foundations as pervasive infiltrators of policy infrastructures in university systems, specifically in public health, and the social sciences. According to Arnove, foundations, on an international level, "help maintain an economic and political order which benefits the ruling-class interests of philanthropists." This claim criticizes foundations for promoting set agendas, serving the interests of industrial capitalism, and acting, in a sense, like "agencies of hegemony, imposing cultural imperialism on minorities and subordinate classes at home and abroad."

Berman (1983) questioned the role of foundations such as Carnegie, Rockefeller, and Ford as proponents of US hegemony overseas, highlighting the important role played by the foundations in their support of universities "whose activities help to legitimate the system of state capitalism." More recently, Brison (2005) discussed the hegemonic influence of US foundations over Canada's higher education institutions where "scholars were not free to pursue the full range of intellectual curiosity" (p. 12). In his study of Rockefeller, Ford, and Carnegie, Parmar (2002) concludes that foundations developed international knowledge networks and influenced the research agenda "to build policy-relevant research and training institutions that would produce graduates with skills and ideas that fit Western notions of development." Parmar (2012) even suggests that a "globally hegemonic mindset is revealed in the foundations' funding strategies" in Africa.[5] For this scholar, US foundations in the 1960s were engaged in "developing and implementing a hegemonic project involving the state, corporations, and intellectual elites."

However, do US foundations always foster a pro-Western agenda? Do their grant recipients perceive their interventions as hegemonic? A simple "yes" to these questions would not account for the complexity of the grantor–grantee relationship. As Kenneth Prewitt describes in Hammack and Heydemann (2009), institutions such as foundations have no overt coercive powers, "they cannot tax, regulate, legislate or perform the functions of the State"[6] nor do they offer profits or return on investment like commercial institutions. Yet, the question of their influence on society and in the world is important and has been commented upon extensively (Berman 1983; Hammack and Heydemann 2009; Parmar 2012).

In focusing on whether or not US independent foundations' involvement with African universities constitutes a hegemonic influence, most studies tend to discount the dynamics that operate between both sets of institutions. Taking a different route for researching the role of US foundations abroad is not only necessary to avoid the limitations of a hegemonic interpretation, it also offers the potential to unveil new ground for research on the field of educational philanthropy. For instance, Nigerian scholar Christiana Tamuno concludes, "There is nothing wrong in incorporating into the Nigerian university foreign models of education."[7] While Tamuno acknowledges that not all programs related to the development of Ibadan University carried out by the Carnegie Corporation of New York, The Rockefeller Foundation, and Ford Foundation were successful, her empirical study, which included scores of interviews with administrators, faculty, and students at the University of Ibadan, did not uncover any form of hegemonic control associated with the grants received from foundations. She also suggests that these foundations were legitimate as active participants in Nigeria's higher education development. Moreover, the reorganization of educational systems to improve productivity and cost efficiency may impede social mobility as this was suggested by scholars who interpreted the work of foundations with a clearly ideological and hegemonic lens (see, for instance, Darknell in Arnove 1980). However, one cannot make inferences about foundations' motives solely based on these possible effects.

In a review of Arnove's *Philanthropy and Cultural Imperialism*, Paul DiMaggio (1983) commented on the study's functionalist bias as one that "blinds the authors, at times, to the reality of organizational life in foundations: too often, foundations are conceived as purposeful and rational unitary actors." This tendency, according to DiMaggio, is reinforced by the absence of interviews with officers, grantees, and unsuccessful applicants, in addition to an overreliance on official documents. DiMaggio concludes that much of the discussion of foundation behavior in the less developed world suggests the "thoughtless application of Western models, rather than conscious efforts to impose hegemony." He states that: "In some instances, as in African education, the importation of Western ideologies may well have increased the autonomy of local university systems. While such organizational factors as problemistic search or dependence on routine information channels are clearly conservative in their effects, a greater recognition of the role of organizational concerns and internal conflict would have helped the authors consider the limits and opportunities for foundation autonomy from capital or the state." Thus, it makes sense to explore foundations by bypassing the hegemonic discourse and examining their work through an institutional lens, particularly with those seeking to impact a field as complex as higher education in Africa. This approach has the advantage of questioning how internal and external mechanisms influence foundations' actions, and which environmental forces legitimize their role, and constrain their resources and strategies.

Legitimizing the Role of Foundations in African Higher Education

The discourse surrounding the priorities of higher education in Africa is set in a battlefield where grantors and grantees must not only mediate their conflicting perspectives but also contend with national contexts that do not necessarily encourage the development of universities. Much to their credit, American foundations have succeeded in increasing the visibility and importance of higher education on the African continent. To some extent, their action parallels the changes that they brought to the field of higher education in the USA a hundred years ago, when most university professors either lived in poverty or were wealthy enough to embrace the profession without consequences, and university facilities hardly qualified as satisfactory places of learning. In the last decade, American foundations have helped shift the national priorities of African countries toward the field of higher education by convincing international funders and national governments that higher education is the key to economic development. This has resulted in larger investments from all stakeholders and a shift toward modernization, institutionalization, and internationalization in African universities. This has not always been the case, as is confirmed by a World Bank report on strategies for the stabilization and revitalization of African universities: "Universities and the governments that support them exist in an uneasy and sometimes adversarial relationship across much of Sub-Saharan Africa. The principal sources of this tension are governments' perception of the university community as a frequent locus of criticism and political opposition, the increased involvement of governments in university affairs, and the inability of governments to provide for the financial needs of universities on a sustainable basis."[8] Similarly, national governments can obstruct foreign foundations working toward revitalizing universities and institutionalizing the field of higher education. Indeed, a foreign foundation's strategies are often incompatible with the local government's policies. In this context, legitimacy is granted as long as foundations are perceived to be acting accountably, by representing the interests of their beneficiaries (e.g., universities) without raising issues that would put them in conflict with national governments. The legitimacy of international philanthropy is therefore formed within a complex network of universities, governments, and foundations, each of which holds a different perspective and set of expectations. When analyzing the connection between institutional priorities and the process of legitimation, it is important to examine the variations between the institutional discourses of universities. In order to do so, this study assessed 14 universities which benefitted from the PHEA's support between 2000 and 2010. Interviews with individuals who were associated with these institutions revealed the priorities of each of these universities, which primarily revolved around the issues of institutional sustainability, competition for resources, and policies and national contexts. Arguably, it is by meeting the needs of universities that foundations would both receive validation for their choices and legitimacy for their role.

Partnership foundations gained legitimacy by helping universities become less dependent on external funding—specifically by leveraging funds and support from national governments and making the case for universities in national contexts. This point is clearly illustrated in the following quote from an interview with the faculty of the Higher Education Research and Advocacy Network in Africa (HERANA):

> It's a pity that the Partnership itself has dissolved because I think that the small gains that it did achieve needed to be built on, both in terms of up-scaling, because unfortunately higher education is still not a priority for governments. They don't seem to have bought into this notion that higher education is absolutely vital for the development of poor countries... We need to constantly hammer it, and I think that's where the foundations could have helped us, the Partnership could have helped us in pushing these things, because unfortunately although the higher education people both in the sector in universities and in the policymaking domain, they understand education but they don't understand development.[9]

The Partnership is described as capable of making higher education a priority for governments and policy-makers, particularly by demonstrating the positive impact of higher education on development. In the eyes of the HERANA faculty, foundations had the ability and legitimacy to change the place of higher education in these countries. In the quote, foundations are seen as having the right amount of expertise in higher education and in development, as opposed to policy-makers and local higher education leaders. However, it appears that the Partnership did not do enough, as the faculty called for the foundations to engage more effectively with governments in order to achieve sustainable results. Additionally, not all grantees believed in the ability of foundations to improve higher education in Africa. In an interview conducted in June 2010, a vice-chancellor of the University of Cape Town explains that foundations are ultimately limited by governments' political will to create this change, or the lack thereof:

> After their contribution, there is nothing that the foundations can do because they have contributed to raising the issue and focusing the minds of involved groups of people. Beyond that, it's really up to the universities involved and their respective governments to do something about it, and that is where the challenge still remains.[10]

This quotes highlights legitimacy as much as it does sustainability. If governments are not interested in supporting universities, do foreign foundations have a right or duty to intervene, or are they overstepping their bound? In this case, political will remains the main obstacle to the long-term development of higher education in Africa, despite the best efforts of American foundations and their grantees.

Partnership interviewees also acknowledged that the foundations did not engage enough with governments to make the case for higher education, and many observed that they would have made this case in a different way. In an interview conducted in July 2011, Suzanne Grant Lewis, describes the gulf between foundations and national governments:

> Basically these seven foundations had almost nothing to do with government. And that's not unusual for foundations. Their view is it's not our forte. We might make grants to people who work on policy advocacy or policy change, but we don't engage in that directly. We are private funders. We very rarely interacted with national or local government.[11]

Indeed, governments were not the direct targets of the foundations' advocacy for higher education development. As private entities, foundations specialize in institutional rather than political relationships, and so prefer to work with institutions rather than governments. The Partnership foundations' limited engagement with local governments reflects the general tendency of US foundations to keep the government at arm's length, even though the cooperation of the public and private spheres is key to ensuring the sustainable development of universities while decreasing their dependency on foreign donors. In most cases, the Partnership's foundations cast a watchful eye over their beneficiaries. They offered continuous support to some of their grantees, who, in turn, legitimated their presence and acknowledged their contributions. The following quote from Mamman Aminu Ibrahim, convener of the Nigeria ICT Forum of Partnership Institutions demonstrates the continued involvement of foreign foundations in institutional matters:

> We always refer to Carnegie and MacArthur as granddads because they were involved at every stage, even the discussion that started the forum, all activities, they were financing and supporting.[12]

Although Ibrahim's comment suggests a certain degree of dependency between foundations and grantees—Carnegie and MacArthur's involvement throughout these organizations' history is described in patriarchal terms—it also highlights a close relationship between grantors and grantees developed over the years with a degree of trust and mutual understanding beneficial to both parties.

Grantees also expected foundations to behave in certain ways. For instance, it was expected that foundations would pay attention to all the actors involved in areas targeted by their initiatives, as Catherine Ngugi, a faculty member at Makerere University in Uganda, suggests:

> Very little work is done by foundations or the universities themselves on the value of in-kind contributions. It is important for the institutions and the foundations to be thinking about it. If foundations really want to show their commitment

to higher education, it behooves them to have an understanding of what other people working on the same area are doing.[13]

These remarks underline the grantees' expectation for foundations to act within and with the community they purport to be serving, involving people on the ground in higher-level decision-making. Foundations must be a part of the university ecosystem, and avoid funding from afar. The foundations' commitment to higher education in Africa depends on this consideration, as does their legitimacy in the eyes of their stakeholders. Grantees gained from the process of funding and were closely monitored by grantors, as Muhammad Y. Bello, a faculty member at Bayero University, confirms:

> So for me the grant served two purposes. First there is the common African proverb, that it is better to teach somebody how to fish than to give that person a fish for the day. The MacArthur grant for us went a step further. It provided us with a fish. It provided us with the money to do a number of things, but it also taught us to source money from other places—based on our experience and sometimes using that as leverage.[14]

Bello clearly accepts MacArthur's role as a solution provider, as a trainer, as a fundraising adviser, and as a funder. In exchange, the grantor is fully accepted in its role. The legitimation mechanism put in place is central to the relationship, and serves both parties.

The influence of foundations on African universities is important, and has multiplying effects for both grantors and grantees when the relationship is successful. This rapport is also the most powerful process for legitimization that impact-seeking philanthropists seek. Dr. Monica Karuhanga Berehao, a professor in the Department of Agricultural Studies at Makerere University, describes this mutually beneficial relationship with Carnegie Corporation of New York:

> Carnegie made [the relationship] move beyond policy statements to something being done. Carnegie has helped us have something on the ground, which we can. It has laid ground for other donors to see the importance and relevance to push these initiatives forward.[15]

On one hand, Carnegie's support lifted several initiatives from words into action. On the other, these initiatives also served as examples to convince other funders to support similar activities. This ensured Carnegie's legitimacy and multiplied the impact of these initiatives by leveraging other funders. In the follow passage, Wilhelmina Tete Mensah, the director of the Gender Mainstreaming Directorate at the University of Education in Winneba, Ghana, explains how a Carnegie-backed initiative—the funding of gender studies programs in African universities—was legitimized within the recipient institution:

> Previously the university had very little in terms of gender... thanks to Carnegie's support we have some books and journals in the library... I believe that through

this gradually we were able to build the interest of people in the area of gender
...[as] a legitimate area of study...We hope to be able to establish a department
of gender studies.[16]

Through its relationship with Carnegie, the University of Education at Winneba
moved from being a recipient of resources for gender studies to a proponent
of gender studies as a legitimate area of study. This process of legitimization
enables foundations to expand their efforts beyond a single program or a single
university, with the effects of each grant extending far beyond its original purpose. Carnegie was not the only foundation to benefit from these legitimation
processes. Arguably, all foundations did. The following example provided by
Dr. Francis Egbokhare at the University of Ibadan illustrates how John D. and
Catherine T. MacArthur Foundation pushed distance learning as an area that
became central to the University:

> One great thing happened with the funding of the MacArthur Foundation. The
> Distance Learning Center was identified as a place that had potential because it was
> part of the package of the initial grant that was actually given in 2002 as part of the
> funding fee. So that in itself created or put the Distance Learning on the University's
> priority as one of the flagships, something that the University wanted to showcase.[17]

Like gender studies in the previous example, distance learning went from a
small, relatively marginal program to a flagship at Ibadan thanks to just one
grant from MacArthur. In exchange, the initiative was showcased by the university and copied by other universities. The initiative also became fully legitimate in the process, and even more so when the university became its best
advocate, thus encouraging other universities to follow suit.

The relationship between a funder and a beneficiary was one of power; the
sources of potential conflict were carefully monitored. Establishing trust was
an arduous process, as Carnegie Corporation's of New York former Program
Director Patricia Rosenfield indicates, since both parties were conscious of the
risks of an unequal power-sharing relationship:

> We learned about the concept of working in partnership with the Vice Chancellors,
> or the appropriate person in the field so it's truly a peer to peer relationship, under-
> standing that we have the power relations with the money but they have the power
> relations because they have the institution. There are lines of intersection and then
> being really open to learning and being told 'no, this is not the way to proceed.'[18]

Foundations and universities are described as peers with equal powers in a partnership, with foundations' control of funds on one hand and institutions' control of
infrastructures, programs, and people on the other. There is a status quo as both
partners can gain or lose from the relationship. The learning process described
reflects the necessary trust-building efforts that foundations have to take into consideration. Grantees are also described as having veto powers and the ability to say
no. However, this conversation is also biased as the grantees' necessity will often

push them to say what grantors want to hear. The following excerpt, taken from a 2004 report on the evaluation of the Partnership, confirms this point:

> There were additional concerns that it is all too easy for donors to be told only what grantees think the donors want to hear. Frustrations were expressed by some foundation staff about how difficult it can be to get universities to lead the discourse on priorities, even when they were encouraged by the foundations to do so.[19]

The process was successful at times, as the following comment by Dr. M.L. Luhanga, vice-chancellor of the University of Dar es Salaam confirms: "Foundations should believe in the philosophy of the Partnership for Higher Education in Africa as practiced by Carnegie. It was responsive to the needs of African countries and spearheaded by Vartan Gregorian."[20] This grantee praises the philosophy and approach of the grantor to the point of commending the grantor's leadership. Carnegie's president, Vartan Gregorian, epitomizes his foundation's responsiveness to the needs of African universities, which are not generally prioritized by governments and international funders despite their fast-growing rates of enrollment and research demonstrating higher education's positive impact on economic growth, poverty reduction, national health, and governance. Gregorian's vision and influence were instrumental in making the world see Africa's universities as critical contributors in helping to shape the discussion of the continent's future. The Bandwidth Consortium became the Partnership's signature project. It was generally acknowledged as the foundations' most successful initiative which expanded Internet affordability for universities in Nigeria, Ghana, and Tanzania. This example illustrates how these foundations paid attention to the specific needs of their grantees, transforming their grantmaking policies into strategic philanthropy focused on initiatives which offered promising impact. In accomplishing this entrepreneurial task and serving the long-term interests of their grantees, the foundations worked for social investment beyond grantmaking. They established an equal partnership with universities, non-profit organizations, corporations, and academic networks. This approach helped the foundations address concerns regarding their accountability, transparency, and professionalism, while acquiring legitimacy and the space to negotiate their own undertakings.

In lieu of hegemonic dependency, which often transpires in the literature on US foundations abroad, this study analyzes the relationship of US foundations and African universities as a virtuous circle of serving and being served, highlighting a mechanism that provided legitimacy to grantors and leverage to grantees. Makerere University in Uganda offers a good example of this phenomenon. In 1963, Makerere became the University of East Africa, offering courses leading to general degrees from the University of London. The special relationship with the University of London came to an end in 1970, and the University of East Africa instituted its own degree programs. On July 1, 1970, Makerere became an independent national university, offering undergraduate and postgraduate courses leading to its own degrees. Carnegie first initiated grants to Makerere University in 1937 and supported a variety of programs at the university. Between 2000 and 2010, Makerere University received $42 million from Carnegie Corporation of New York, The Rockefeller Foundation, Ford Foundation, and The Andrew W. Mellon Foundation through the Partnership and from other donors. Today, Makerere is a fee-based institution whose ambition is to become "a center of academic excellence, providing world-class teaching, research and service relevant to sustainable development needs of society," detailed in its mission statement. Hegemony-oriented theorists would argue that Makerere's relationship with US foundations pushed the university toward an American model. However, Makerere's shift toward high tuition and globalist ambition is a result of the university's exchange of legitimacy with foreign funders. The process of integrating an international dimension into the purpose and delivery of its education came from the university's interaction with donors. Its success in attracting large foundation gifts led Makerere to become a standard for Africa's other universities, which, in turn, replicate Makerere's strategy in order to compete. Makerere has also used its fundraising success to legitimize its autonomy from state control, and advance to new levels (Court 1999). Universities such as Makerere act strategically to manage their resource dependencies. The dynamic interaction and evolution of universities with foreign donors is explained by this mechanism of inter-organizational legitimation. Hence, external resource dependence affects both internal and trans-organizational dynamics but can be maneuvered to a universities' advantage.

The foundations' preference for some institutions over others can be seen as an issue of legitimation, as some institutions are better positioned to legitimize the foundations' initiatives. Thus, legitimation becomes a question of power. An institution's ability to legitimize an issue is determined by its relative social, political, and economic power. The nature of power in inter-organizational relationships led grantees to believe that acting in the interests of more powerful partners was consistent with their own interests. Considering the Partnership's environmental context in Africa along with the importance of legitimacy, it can be observed that collaborative and environmental factors contribute to legitimizing the foundations' role and goals in higher education in Africa. The Partnership's advocacy component, in the eyes of their constituents, provided legitimacy to the foundations because they strove to achieve policy outcomes that reflected the general commitment to environmental principles and practices that their grantees valued. Resource-dependent universities must interact with other institutions in their environment to acquire needed resources. Problems arise not merely because organizations are dependent on their environment, but because this environment is not dependable. The need for resources—financial and physical resources as well as information—makes universities potentially dependent on the external environment as a supplier of these resources. The environment, including local actors, is a strong factor influencing inter-organizational variation. This view suggests that universities are embedded in networks of interdependencies and social relationships. As they try to alter their environments, they become subject to new and different constraints as the very patterns of interdependence change. African universities attempt to manage the constraints and uncertainty that result from the need to acquire resources from their environment. Because of external constraints on revenue and autonomy, decision-making organizations possess both the desire and the ability to negotiate their position within those constraints using a variety of tactics.

Notes

1. Lester Salamon (in Hewa and Stapleton 2005), p. 137.
2. Peter Frumkin (in Hewa and Stapleton 2005), p. 113.
3. Prewitt (in Prewitt et al. 2006), p. 29.
4. Gaudiani (2003), p. 44.
5. Parmar (2012), p. 178.
6. Hammack and Heydemann (2009), p. viii.
7. Tamuno (1986), p. 137.
8. Saint (1992), p. xiv.
9. Transcript of June 2010 Interview with Faculty, HERANA, South Africa. Megan Lindow personal archives.
10. Transcript of June 2010 Transcript of Interview with vice-chancellor, University of Cape Town, South Africa. Megan Lindow personal archives.
11. July 8, 2011 interview with Suzanne Grant Lewis, coordinator, PHEA.
12. Transcript of June 2010 interview with Mamman Aminu Ibrahim, convenor of the Nigeria ICT Forum of Partnership Institutions. Megan Lindow personal archives.
13. Transcript of June 2010 interview with Catherine Ngugi, faculty member at Makerere University in Uganda. Megan Lindow personal archives.
14. Transcript of June 2010 interview with Muhammad Y. Bello, faculty member at Bayero University in Nigeria. Megan Lindow personal archives.
15. Transcript of interview with Dr. Monica Karuhanga Berehao. Lecturer in the Department of Agricultural Extension & Innovations Studies, Makerere University. (circa 2010). Megan Lindow personal archives.
16. Transcript of interview with Dr. Wilhelmina Tete Mensah, director, Gender Mainstreaming Directorate at University of Education, Winneba, Ghana (circa 2010). Megan Lindow personal archives.
17. Transcript of interview with Dr. Francis Egbokhare, a Professor in the Department of Linguistics and African Languages, University of Ibadan, Nigeria. (circa 2010) Megan Lindow personal archives.
18. August 19, 2011 interview in New York with Patricia Rosenfield, program director, Carnegie Corporation of New York.
19. Moja et al. (2004), p. 18.
20. Transcript of interview with Dr. M. L. Luhanga Vice-Chancellor, University of Dar es Salaam in Tanzania. Megan Lindow personal archives.

Bibliography

Aldrich, H.E., and C.M. Fiol. 1994. Fools rush in? The institutional context of industry creation. *Organization Studies* 19(4): 645–670.

Anheier, Helmut K., and Toepler, Stefan. 1999. *Private Funds, Public Purpose. Philanthropic Foundations in International Perspective.* New York: Kluwer Academic / Plenum Publishers.

Arnove, Robert F. 1980. *Philanthropy and cultural imperialism: The foundations at home and abroad.* Boston: G.K. Hall.

Au bonheur des autres. Anthropologie de l'aide humanitaire (For Their Own Good. Anthropology of Humanitarian Aid), Societe d'Ethnologie, 2005 and re-published by Armand Colin in 2009 Ethnologie francaise/Presses universitaires de France, 2011); La sante globale, nouveau laboratoire de l'aide international? (Global Health; A New Laboratory for International Aid?) with L. Vidal, Armand Colin/Tiers Monde, 2013

Bacchetti, Ray, and Thomas Ehrlich. 2007. *Reconnecting education and foundations. Turning good intentions into educational capital.* Stanford: Carnegie Foundation for the Advancement of Teaching.

Berman, Edward H. 1971. American influence on African education: The role of the Phelps-Stokes fund's education commissions. *Comparative Education Review* 15(2): 132–145.

——— 1983. *The ideology of philanthropy. The influence of the Carnegie, Ford, and Rockefeller foundations on American foreign policy.* Albany: SUNY Press.

Brinkerhoff, Derick W. 2005. *Organisational legitimacy, capacity and capacity development.* ECDPM Discussion Paper 58A. Maastricht: ECDPM.

Brison, Jeffrey D. 2005. *Rockefeller, Carnegie, and Canada: American philanthropy and the arts and letters in Canada.* Montreal: McGill-Queen's University Press.

Bullock, Mary B. 1973/1944. *The Rockefeller foundation in China: Philanthropy, Peking Union Medical College, and public health.* Doctoral Dissertation, Stanford University.

Clotfelter, Charles T., and Thomas Ehrlich. 1999. *Philanthropy and the nonprofit sector in a changing America.* Bloomington: Indiana University Press.

Court, David. 1999. *Financing higher education in Africa: Makerere, the quiet revolution.* Joint report of the World Bank and the Rockefeller foundation. Washington, DC

Dedrick, John Robert. 1997. *Civil society and private philanthropy: A study of philanthropic foundations in the United States.* Doctoral dissertation, The State University of New Jersey, New Brunswick.

Deephouse, David L., and Suzanne M. Carter. 2005. An examination of differences between organizational legitimacy and organizational reputation. *Journal of Management Studies* 42: 2.

DiMaggio, Paul. 1983. Review: A jaundiced view of philanthropy. Philanthropy and cultural imperialism: The foundations at home and Abroad by Robert F. Arnove. *Comparative Education Review* 27(3): 442–445.

Dowie, Mark. 2002. *American foundations: An investigative history.* Cambridge: MIT Press.

Fleishman, Joel. 2007. *The foundation: A great American secret; How private wealth is changing the world.* New York: Public Affairs.

Friedman, Lawrence, and Mark D. Mcgarvie (eds.). 2003. *Charity, philanthropy and civility in American history.* Cambridge: Cambridge University Press.

Gaudiani, Claire. 2003. *The greater good: How philanthropy drives The American economy and can save capitalism.* New York: Times Books.

Gregory, Keneth. 2000. *Engineering social reform: The rise of the Ford Foundation and Cold War liberalism, 1908–1959.* Doctoral dissertation, New York University.

Hammack, David C., and Steven Heydemann (eds.). 2009. *Globalization, philanthropy, and civil society. Projecting institutional logics abroad.* Bloomington: Indiana University Press.

Hewa, Soma, and Darwin Stapleton. 2005. *Globalization, philanthropy, and civil society.* New York: Springer.

Karoff, Peter. 2008. *The world we want. New dimensions in philanthropy and social change.* Lanham: Altamira Press.

Kiger, Joseph. 2000. *Philanthropic foundations in the twentieth century.* Westport: Greenwood Press.

———. 2008. *Philanthropists, and foundation globalization.* New Brunswick: Transaction Publishers.

Moja T., J. Reddy, and A. White. (2004). *Evaluation of the Partnership for Higher Education in Africa.* Unpublished.

Nielsen, Waldemar A. 2004. *Golden donors: A new anatomy of the great foundations.* New Brunswick: Transaction.

Parmar, Inderjeet. 2002. American foundations and the development of international knowledge networks. *Global Networks* 2(1): 13–30.

———. 2012. *Foundations of the American century. The Ford, Carnegie, and Rockefeller foundations in the rise of American power.* New York: Columbia University Press.

Prewitt, K., M. Dogan, S. Heydemann, and S. Toepler. 2006. *The legitimacy of philanthropic foundations: United States and European perspectives.* New York: Russell Sage Foundation Publications.

Roelofs, Joan. 2003. *Foundations and public policy: The mask of pluralism.* Albany: SUNY Press.

Rosenbaum, Thomas E. 1989. Rockefeller philanthropies in revolutionary Russia. *Rockefeller Archive Center Newsletter.*

Saint, William S. 1992. *Universities in Africa: Strategies for stabilization and revitalization.* Technical Paper No.194. Technical Department, Africa Region. Washington, DC: World Bank.

Sanborn, Cynthia, and Felipe Portocarrero. 2005. *Philanthropy and social change in Latin America.* Cambridge: Harvard University Press.

Tamuno, Christiana. 1986. *The roles of the Rockefeller foundation, Ford foundation and Carnegie Corporation in the development of the University of Ibadan 1962–1978.* Doctoral dissertation, The University of Pittsburgh.

Tournès, Ludovic. 2002. La diplomatie culturelle de la fondation Ford. Les éditions Intercultural Publications (1952–1959), *XXe siècle.* Revue d'histoire, pp. 65–77.

Wormser, René. 1958. *Foundations: Their power and influence.* New York: The Devin-Adair Company.

CHAPTER 8

The Discourse on Priorities Among Donors

There remain several issues regarding universities' dependency on external sources of funding, particularly with respect to the inequity of partnerships between richly endowed foundations in the USA and resource-seeking institutions in the global south. The problem is especially severe for foundations interacting with universities in Africa. These partnerships grew out of a context of scarce resources, in which the research agendas of grantees did not always match those of the grantors but were modified in order to access available funds. In addition, competition for resources existed among higher education institutions in Africa. There was a necessity for all involved to pressure national governments to be more responsive to universities' needs. This discussion extends beyond the role of foundations in developing countries or their influence on universities in Africa. It concerns all types of non-African international donors, development agencies, and philanthropic organizations that seek to play a role in the development of Africa while setting priorities and strategies with limited participation from Africans. This exclusion of precisely those whom these institutions claim to serve raises many significant questions. For instance, can US foundations embrace Africa's development on Africa's terms? Do African universities have ownership over their participation in US foundations' strategies for Africa? What legitimizes the role of US foundations in African higher education? The discourse on priorities in African higher education is placed in a contested terrain, where grantors and grantees not only negotiate one another's perspectives but also contend with inhospitable national contexts. In certain African countries, governments do not necessarily encourage the development of universities or international donors who are not overtly cooperative. This chapter examines the discourse on priorities set by developers and the pressure for durable and sustainable outcomes.

© The Editor(s) (if applicable) and The Author(s) 2016
F. Jaumont, *Unequal Partners*, Philanthropy and Education,
DOI 10.1057/978-1-137-59348-1_8

THE RHETORIC OF CAPACITY BUILDING

The literature on non-profit organizations and development studies suggests that organizations need legitimacy for durability and sustainability. If foundations behave according to this rule, the Partnership's foundations must have seen capacity building as an important mechanism to maximize legitimacy, particularly as they strove to generate transformations impacting the institutionalization of higher education organizations in Africa. In the context of higher education development, capacity building is geared toward developing an organization's management structures, processes and procedures, institutional and legal framework, human resources, and access to information. In the case of universities in Africa, capacity building is an important focus for international donors who seek to target organizations that need support for change and lack the necessary funding, expertise, and training to sustain their institutional growth. Brinkerhoff (2005) notes that the connections between legitimacy, institutionalization, and sustainability point toward legitimacy as a significant element of capacity building. Thus, by identifying the connection between legitimacy and capacity building, the story of the Partnership can shed light on prominent institutional legitimation forces.

Comparing the Partnership's foundations' grantmaking strategies for higher education in Africa reveals a diversity of approaches. However, during the Partnership years, the seven foundations' approaches to the development of African higher education varied immensely. Carnegie Corporation of New York supported university revitalization and transformation and made large institutional grants to eight major university grantees. It also had a strong focus on enhancing women's opportunities in nine universities. Ford Foundation invested on the frontlines of social change by advancing the work of local visionaries. It also carried out the African Higher Education Initiative (AHEI) through regional offices. John D. and Catherine T. MacArthur Foundation focused on institutional strengthening of four universities in Nigeria and one in Madagascar. Its work in a number of areas, such as conservation and sustainable development, human rights, and population and reproductive health was largely done through the academic institutions and research networks it supported. The Rockefeller Foundation built up African research capacity in agriculture, health, and economics. The foundation supported regional postgraduate training and research networks for future researchers and professionals (agricultural economists, modern crop breeders, and public health practitioners). Makerere University in Uganda was its major grant recipient. The William and Flora Hewlett Foundation focused on population, education, global development, and philanthropy. It had a mandate to solve social and environmental problems and trained the next generation of African population scientists, supporting individuals' reproductive health rights, and developing open educational resources. The Andrew W. Mellon Foundation sought to strengthen South African universities and the production of excellent scholars. The foundation supported academic and research program development, postgraduate training, faculty development, and the development of archival collections. And finally, The Kresge Foundation worked on developing infrastructure through matching grants, while helping grantees improve their strategic planning, advancement, and fundraising, particularly in South Africa. The interest of the foundations in institutional development was expressed in different ways, such as through infrastructure development, organization strengthening, research capacity expansion, revitalization, sustainable development, advancement, fundraising, or strategic planning. When describing what united the Partnership's founding members, Joyce Moock, lead program officer for the Partnership, stated the following:

> Some of the foundations lean towards intellectual energy in research, research for the important point of producing new knowledge; others are more interested in doing that but also in the conversion of that knowledge into something more practical and operational, a translational form. The four foundations [Carnegie, Rockefeller, Ford, MacArthur] have a long history in these kinds of things, but it runs very deep into the grain of these institutions, into their DNA if you will. In other words, the nature of these large, private international foundations has a lot of deep capacity building. Now, maybe not in agricultural or in health or whatever some may not have a program called higher education, but if you look into their individual programs you'll find that elements of capacity building, whether in fellowships or in developing institutions, are very prominent.[1]

Here, the foundations' interest in institutional development and capacity building is described as part of the foundations' core function. With the addition of new members, the priorities of the Partnership remained focused on institutional development. In fact, this was reinforced by institutional affinities and similarities, and the meshing of values among partners. The Partnership shaped the foundations' actions around the goals of resource expansion. This would serve the purpose of impacting African universities and academic networks with greater strength. This assertion underscores the myth of capacity building as an element of mimetic affinity among foundations; a ceremonial enactment of high-impact decisions indicating a shared desire to create greater returns on investment at work in the world of large, international foundations. Arguably, the myth of capacity building and the ceremonial act of impact investing gave foundations enough justification and collective endorsement to eventually maximize legitimacy.

While foundations conformed to the myth of building capacity, they also designed and promoted a discourse of capacity building to support this strategy. Core functions were defined in the language of capacity builders. The foundations would solve challenges faced by African universities through a focus on providing financial support. This concentrated on the universities' capital infrastructure, lowering costs through economies of scale, positioning higher education as a responsible partner in building democratic societies, triggering public policy reform, increasing access and gender equity, and encouraging inter-institutional collaboration. According to its mission statement, the Partnership capitalized on the distinctive contribution of each foundation through shared learning. It enhanced the ability of grantmakers to support sustainable improvements in university performance. The Partnership's reports underscore that the foundations tried to "test and demonstrate the best that philanthropy had to offer by pooling knowledge and strategies." It aimed to provide "balanced emphases on the academic and the practical, thus enabling universities to become more robust intellectual institutions that can successfully produce a new generation of scholars, analysts, scientists, technologists, teachers, public servants, and entrepreneurs." The following graph presents the distribution of grants per recipient type and confirms this objective (Fig. 8.1).

Analyzing foundation spending the Partnership's grant nomenclature even reflected the preference for capacity building that directed the foundations' grantmaking. The foundations unfolded their capacity building strategy by focusing on institutional development and structuring ICT. Institutional and capacity development emerged as priorities for each foundation, followed by ICT, which is a form of capacity development itself. Indeed, fiber optic cable and the Bandwidth Consortium project are among the Partnership's capstone achievements. The most significant accomplishment of the Partnership was to provide Internet bandwidth at affordable prices to African universities in desperate need of essential resources for research and teaching. With help from the Partnership, universities in several West African countries formed a consortium to purchase a sixfold increase in bandwidth and provide Internet service at lower rates—a significant first step toward parity in the online world. All participating foundations agreed on supporting the bandwidth initiative though not all foundations funded it. Other areas such as administrative staff development, technical assistance, library support and, to a certain extent, academic research support, could also be counted as capacity building. There was very little specialization in the Partnership; no foundation had a single area of focus. Nevertheless, the approach that dominated the Partnership reveals how

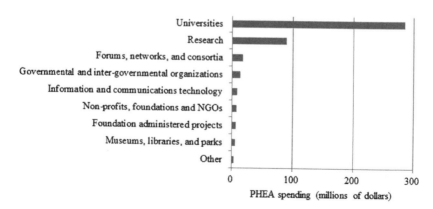

Fig. 8.1   Distribution of grants per recipient type

foundations conform to the myth of capacity building. Capacity building did not solely function as a leveraging process between these foundations. It also worked as a collective rhetoric framing the initiatives of the foundations. In the words of David Court, capacity building helped these foundations reach a consensus, despite the fragmented nature of their collaboration:

> Through a process of self-education the Partners have developed a consensus in their approach to capacity building needs, but in practice each has different emphases in where and how they address training needs. Individually training projects, e.g. Carnegie Women's Fellowship Program, Rockefeller's Makerere decentralization training, and Ford's Fellowships all have different purposes and target groups with the result that capacity building is fragmented.[2]

Thus, capacity building functioned as a ceremonial rite that framed the individual and collective ambitions of the foundations, and rallied foundation representatives around a common goal. This was confirmed by the tremendous good will among the foundation representatives to the PHEA. All were committed to strengthening higher education in Africa and all appeared to believe that their own foundation's grantmaking was improved by the collaboration. The Partnership's actors shared both the myth of capacity building and a desire to legitimize the grantmaking of their own foundation. As such, capacity building was not just a unifying approach among these foundations but it also transformed the objectives of these foundations. The rhetoric of institutionalization prevalent in the Partnership leveraged some legitimacy by conforming to the myths and ceremonial rite of capacity building. In a seminal study, Ira Silvers (2006) suggests looking beyond the rhetoric of philanthropic collaborations. Indeed, the Partnership was not simply a question of rhetoric and conformity with environmental myths; it was also a strategy that generated legitimacy from its influence on the field of African higher education. The following section explores the strategy of influence that the Partnership's members conceived collectively.

Influence Strategy and High-Impact Philanthropy

Given the complexity of the various types of legitimacy, the foundations in the Partnership were unlikely to be in a position to satisfy all participants. Program officers and foundation leaders needed to choose key environmental stakeholders to respond to and avoid the temptation to please everyone. The beneficiaries in Africa have the ability to provide or to withhold legitimacy. Thus, determining which grantee to pay attention to, from the funders' perspective, became an exercise in grantee analysis. Strategies and visions had to be crafted for grantees to allocate their legitimizing resources in favor of the foundations in the Partnership. The amount of effort put into these strategies depended to some extent on what the foundations in the Partnership could accomplish. If the foundations provided the kind of support that was well recognized, valued, and even desired by the recipients, then they would not have needed heavy investment in strategies that sought recognition and buy-in from grantees. The quest for legitimacy would not be as necessary. If, on the other hand, the foundations were engaged in activities that were questionable or deviated significantly from commonly-accepted funding practices, the response from grantees would automatically condemn the poor judgment of the foundations.

Furthermore, defining a common strategy for higher education in Africa appears unrealistically complex. This is challenging even with a fewer number of countries. Thus, applying a common strategy for nine target countries, with an additional expectation of a potential ripple effect on other African countries, indicates the need for more than an over-simplistic understanding of the challenges ahead. It suggests that the Partnership had a different purpose which turned out to be a valuable contribution: advocacy for higher education. Their selection of grantees was achieved along strict principles. The inaugural Partnership meeting took place on November 29, 1999, where historical connections were predominant and membership prerequisites already in motion. To be selected universities had to be good candidates for potential support according to criteria including past and current relationship with the foundations—that is, The Rockefeller Foundation and Makerere University, and Carnegie Corporation of New York and the University of Dar es Salaam. The grantees had to be dedicated to innovation, which also indicated their willingness to reform their institution. Finally, the grantee had to demonstrate its ability as a proponent or participant in social change for the country it served. Furthermore, the Partnership's strategic plan of selecting countries and institutions was based on three proclaimed principles: reform, democratization and political stability. Constructing a strategy around these principles enabled the Partnership to aspire to ambitious goals which sought to lift a continent, foster economic development and influence knowledge production. The Partnership sought to lift the whole higher education system of sub-Saharan Africa. To do so, it selected countries with progressive democratic and liberalized environments, and with universities on the move that could serve as demonstrations of what higher education in Africa could accomplish under the right conditions. Within this framework, each Foundation concentrated on those countries, and universities within them, that fitted with its mission and preferences. The foundations together supported activities that offered high potential for cross-learning and joint problem-solving. Arguably, the arguments supporting this approach are in contradiction with the realities of Africa. The foundations believed they could impact the continent by selecting mostly Commonwealth countries when in fact clear organizational differences existed between each higher education system, particularly systems that were inherited from different colonial influences. Yet, an accomplishment report published by the PHEA stated that the Partnership "directly or indirectly improved conditions for 4.1 million African students enrolled at 379 universities and colleges" during its 10-year existence (2000–2010). This optimistic claim epitomizes the ambitions of the foundations, as the following quote by Joyce Moock from Rockefeller indicates:

There was a sense that... if we did this the right way it would lift the entire educa-tion system on the subcontinent. That really is bizarre sounding with the kind of money we had to spend. What we were looking for were countries with a progres-sive environment. Also, with some important geopolitical recognition we were looking at the universities on the move as well, and we thought if we could put the funds on the right targets, at the right time, these would serve as demonstrations.[3]

The Partnership's official mission was to provide financial support that concen-trated on "universities in countries undergoing systemic public policy reform and strengthening the ability of individual institutions to play their distinctive role within differentiated national systems of higher education; and encourag-ing inter-institutional collaboration." The following passage describes how the foundations envisioned success for their endeavor:

What would success ultimately look like? Selected universities and centers of intel-lectual inquiry will demonstrate ability to promote the free flow of ideas and enlarge the public sphere of their societies. They will evidence effective use of information technology. As part of the national higher education system they will build and transfer a repertoire of skills essential for the development of their societies. They will be part of a global network of imaginative teaching, research and outreach institutions in which creativity is fed through experimentation and shared experiences. They will reflect a quiet revolution in institution building in Africa that can unleash the talents of the continent for the well-being of its people and those beyond its borders.[4]

The success of the Partnership's strategy gravitated around the notion of a quiet revolution in institution building in Africa that could "unleash the talents of the continent." As such more scholarships were offered to encourage stu-dents to pursue higher education degrees, and to give access to more women and minorities.

Arguably, the Partnership's approach to build capacities by focusing on a few relatively strong universities also appears as a contradiction. Selecting weaker universities and applying a capacity building approach to developing them would make more sense. This point is also valid for education schools which foundation presidents did not favor. It also raised some criticism par-ticularly from universities which did not get selected. Makerere University, the University of Dar-es-Salam, and the University of Ghana were among the "winners." As Narciso Matos, former program director at Carnegie stated: "Other universities facing difficulties, and in need of support, would criticize the foundations for creating an exclusive club and not reaching out to other constituencies that were also in need and so on. Of course this was a deliberate choice that we had made, but we were perceived in that light." [5] However, the Partnership's foundations firmly believed in the multiplying potential of their strategy. By selecting grantees with whom they had long-established connec-tions, which some critics could view as a source of dependency, the foundations orchestrated a maximization strategy which was thought to have the potential to influence the African continent.

Concurrently, the Partnership members added an advocacy component to an already intricate mission. The goal was to make the case for higher education to governments, international organizations, and other donors. The donor community included government agencies, foreign development organizations, foundations, and many other funding institutions with a strategy that relied principally on the foundations' power and prestige, and the Partnership's raison d'être and collective strategy, the goal was to influence this community of international developers. To a lesser extent, non-governmental organizations and intergovernmental organizations such as the New Partnership for Africa's Development or the African Union were also targeted by the foundations. For instance, the African Union added the "Harmonize Higher Education in Africa" program, focusing on quality rating mechanism educational publishing, teacher development, and the revitalization of technical and vocational education. The Partnership's strategy served to leverage other players in the field, the notion of leveraging itself adding credit to the Partnership's impact. Outcomes (as different from outputs) are meant to indicate impact, which can be measured only at the level of perceptions and evaluations among key actors within the academic community, higher education institutions and system, governance structures, governments, and intergovernmental agencies in Africa, as well as bilateral and multilateral agencies, donor community, and African studies and international higher education experts and institutions in the USA and Europe. But also relevant is impact upon the four foundations in their work on African higher education. The foundations in the Partnership gained access to discussions on higher education in national and multilateral settings. This was done with a view to maximize their influence. By buying relatively inexpensive seats at the higher education table in African countries of geopolitical importance, in which funding alliances beyond the Partnership were available, the foundations could help bring promising experiments to scale—with cascading effects across the continent. This leveraging dimension was helpful to the foundations. It added to the Partnership's original objectives which sought to generate reform and institutionalize even further the field of higher education in Africa. The foundations were making a collective statement ranking higher education an absolute necessity for the economic development and political strength of a country in a global society. Using their prestige, foundations were able to promote their ideals by advocating the role of higher education in development. This point reinforces the importance of legitimacy in setting the terrain for the production of position statements.

Not everyone agreed with the approach used by the foundations in making position statements and opportunistic advocacy. For some, the Partnership agenda was not focused enough on helping institutions improve. The Partnership's original vision was to support institution building, not advocacy. Some critics questioned the Partnership's overall strategy for expansion in Africa and if the foundations had a vision for coverage after the Partnership ended. For the skeptics, it was not enough to simply state that the Partnership worked in countries undergoing systemic policy reform and in which two or more foundation had programmatic interest. These were conditions for entry, but these conditions did not define the overall strategic objectives for expansion nor would these preconditions be a guide for a less systemic and opportunistic expansion. Expansion was put to the test when the Partnership's mission and purpose were being challenged, particularly when several foundations were undergoing leadership changes or internal review and redirection processes. The Rockefeller Foundation, for instance, had announced its intentions to focus on large problem-solving initiatives such as Africa's Green Revolution. Against this background, the PHEA was pushed to revisit and interrogate its "raison d'être" and comparative advantage, and reinvent itself. Indeed, the landscape for philanthropy had changed and was being interrogated by the intentions announced by players with larger resources, such as Bill Gates and Warren Buffet. From institution building, the Partnership gradually shifted its focus to advocating for the role of higher education in the development of Africa, as the following comment by Tade Aina, program director at Carnegie, confirms:

> The foundations came to valorize higher education… To give value, not even add value, to give value to the importance of higher education institutions in the economic development of African countries. And to not only affect the debate by doing that, to bring money onto the table to demonstrate their interest.[6]

Not only is the notion of value and valorization in the hands of the foundations but it also has a separate yet complementary relationship to money. The relative strategic deployment of funds in this case confirms that foundations benefit from their privileged status to influence a field. The PHEA injected prestige and a light on the higher education system at a time when it was disregarded as being ineffectual and weak. This was valuable.

Influence on the ecology of donors—including government budgets, international organizations, and development agencies—became an indicator for the Partnership's impact. It became a way for foundations to answer questions of accountability. The following comment is from Narciso Matos, Carnegie's former program director:

> Visibility is essential for successful interventions to encourage other African governments, donors and investment agencies to support higher education and to reassure the foundations' trustees and leaders that money is being effectively invested. On the other hand, too much publicity might raise the expectations of other needy institutions and countries, leading policymakers to steer resources away from partnership universities toward other pressing needs not presently addressed by donors.[7]

National governments, foreign investors, and the World Bank were target interlocutors for the foundations' collaborative effort. The Partnership, in terms of the US and to some extent European policy-makers, worked hard to put the issue of higher education back on the table. The Partnership coincided with reengagement on the part of the World Bank in the field of higher education in Africa after a period of moving away from all kinds of funding to universities and academic networks. The Partnership's advocacy focus is described as having successfully established higher education in Africa as a priority for policymakers and international funders. The World Bank and the Mozambique Ministry of Higher Education appear as Partnership targets that were reached. The Partnership could rightly claim that in Mozambique, it did help develop Mozambique's strategic plan for the development of higher education which over time evolved into the framework for the establishment of 20 different universities in the country. The partnership was very instrumental in helping the then ministry for higher education, science, and technology, to spearhead the process of thinking about higher education in Africa. Eventually the World Bank did approve a major grant to support higher education in Mozambique. In this case, the Partnership played a significant role. The Partnership helped a government spearhead the process of thinking about higher education in Africa and gives itself credit for leveraging a World Bank grant to Mozambique. Finding credit and accountability in their grantees' success is a recurrent theme in the discourse of foundation officers; it is also a way to find legitimacy, particularly within a strategy of influence that is hard to measure otherwise. The goals of these funders were to place higher education in Africa on the priority list of donors and national governments, and leverage support from them while making them recognize the contributions of higher education to the economic development of Africa. In several instances, the World Bank appeared as the Foundations' adversary. Although the World Bank created a specific department for collaboration between the Bank and foundations in order to capitalize on the influx of cash and ideas generated by private foundations, partnering with the World Bank was not the foundations' priority, as it often meant time-consuming efforts at negotiating memoranda of understanding and legal documentation for partnerships. The World Bank saw partnerships with foundations as important in order to "gain knowledge and experience in best practices, research and information related to their specific country knowledge and sector expertise; to share information in order to foster complementary work; and to deepen development work through consultation on corporate priorities such as country and regional assistance strategies." The Bank designed a framework for its collaboration with foundations which saw foundations as complementary to the World Bank's activities. Indeed, the World Bank values partnerships with foundations in the development of poverty reduction strategy with framework of the Millennium Development Goals. The World Bank supported initiatives that were carried out by the foundations as far as they were complementary to the Bank's initiatives, such as research pilots, evaluations, strategies, seminars, and conferences. Paradoxically, the foundations in the Partnership were reluctant to collaborate with the World Bank, while hoping to leverage the Bank's funding potential. The Partnership foundation generally agreed that maximizing the information flow while minimizing formal association would be the most politic way of proceeding, especially given the combination in some countries of the problematic standing of the bank and the politicized nature of higher education. One consequence of this lack of active collaboration between the foundations in the Partnership and other organizations like the World Bank, the African Development Bank, or European foundations is that the opportunity for the Partnership to leverage support for higher education in Africa was never taken advantage of. Nonetheless, higher education in Africa is back on the agenda for many organizations, and the Partnership foundations deserve some credit for their efforts at generating some motivation and some acceleration, and hopefully a strong direction, among all higher education developers and governments alike. They should receive some credit for coming in when they did at the turn of the twenty-first century. Would it have happened anyway if they had not come in?

Notes

1. June 24, 2011 phone interview with Joyce Moock, former associate vice-president, The Rockefeller Foundation, New York.
2. September 29, 2011 phone interview with David Court, former program officer for The Rockefeller Foundation.
3. June 24, 2011 interview with Joyce Moock, associate vice-president, The Rockefeller Foundation.
4. November 10, 2004. Core Statement of the Partnership for Higher Education in Africa. PHEA.
5. September 9, 2011 phone interview with Narciso Matos, former program director, Carnegie Corporation of New York.
6. September 26, 2011 interview with Tade Aina, program director, Carnegie Corporation of New York.
7. September 9, 2011, phone interview with Narciso Matos, former program director, Carnegie Corporation of New York.

Bibliography

Brinkerhoff, Derick W. 2005. *Organisational legitimacy, capacity and capacity development*. ECDPM Discussion Paper 58A. Maastricht: ECDPM.
Silver, Ira. 2006. *Unequal partnerships. Beyond the rhetoric of philanthropic collaboration*. New York: Routledge.

CHAPTER 9

Legitimacy in an Unequal Partnership

Diverging perspectives between grantors and grantees can often have a bearing on the alignment of funding priorities and strategic goals. This difference in perspectives between US grantmakers and their beneficiaries in target universities in Africa is worth examining further, as it is precisely at this point of divergence that legitimacy is created, leveraged, managed, maximized, or withheld. This locus is both a controllable and malleable source of legitimation as well as an indispensable resource for impact-seeking organizations. In order to establish the connection between personal interactions and legitimacy formation in the PHEA, it is relevant to first identify the variations between the discourse of its actors and beneficiaries. Starting from individual perspectives, this chapter examines these divergences by comparing grantor and grantee viewpoints. When examined comparatively, these viewpoints illustrate the importance of a range of internal or external factors on institutions, as well as the mechanisms of convergence and divergence among participating institutions and among individual actors. Although the Partnership was the sum of the individuals that composed it, these individuals were tasked with fulfilling collective goals of the Partnership, the interests of their respective institution, and their own perspectives as active participants. Several testimonies highlighted below present a contrast among grantors and grantees, as some points of views diverged significantly among the two groups.

Once the divergence between the perspectives of funders and beneficiaries on the needs and priorities of higher education institutions in Africa has been established, it becomes relevant to question the level of negotiation that this divergence must have produced. Reconciling the priorities of foundations with the expectations of their grantees was a concern shared by all actors. Interactions between grantors and grantees in the PHEA were therefore instrumental in defining the foundations' strategies. Indeed, the perspectives of university vice-chancellors, administrators, researchers, and even students in Africa were taken into account by the Partnership foundations right from the start of the initiative. According

© The Editor(s) (if applicable) and The Author(s) 2016   111
F. Jaumont, *Unequal Partners*, Philanthropy and Education,
DOI 10.1057/978-1-137-59348-1_9

to Frumkin (2006), grantmakers no longer aim to keep grant recipients at arm's length, separate, and unequal. Instead, they seek to foster engagement and greater equity between funder and grantee. In order to legitimate their actions, foundations need to change the basic terms of power sharing with grantees, particularly if these grantees are in a developing stage. There is an inevitable asymmetry of power when a well-established institution gives money to a less endowed one. However, collaboration and consultation can create configurations of power sharing that do not have predefined limits, particularly in a context of unequal relationships between large US foundations and institutions in the global south. Foundations know that the participation of grantees in setting the agenda for funding is the source of good grantmaking and a factor of success. A number of studies and reports on donor collaboration stress this point.[1] With their claim to serve the common good, foundations are validated for their participation in a category of organizations accepted as pursuing communally valuable goals. This is different from perception and evaluation based on any specific results achieved. In international development, foundations capitalize on the legitimacy accorded to the non-profit and voluntary sector to add significance and precedence to certain causes.

This heightened interest in consultation and power sharing should be interpreted as a positive trend that benefits all actors involved. In the PHEA, grantees' increased opportunities for involvement and participation were encouraged by the foundations who underscored the necessity of including their beneficiaries in the decision-making process. However, many differences of perspective prevailed between grantees and Partnership funders, as illustrated by the following comment by Andrea Johnson, program officer of the Carnegie Corporation of New York:

> We wanted to be able to bring those vice chancellors together and have some very stimulating, visionary conversations. It turns out that in universities where it's hard even to keep the lights on; they're not really thinking long term vision for higher education. They're thinking about 'I need to have enough money available that I can keep the lights on.' So we were always disappointed with the quality of the participation of the higher education leaders.[2]

The desire to create a fruitful exchange of views was shared by all grantors as part of the Partnership's encompassing approach and philosophy. Despite the existing divergence described above, reconciling the perspectives of foundations with those of their beneficiaries was a common concern among the program officers interviewed. It is clear, however, that a constant dialogue was necessary, not only to conduct good grantmaking on the part of foundations but also to obtain some validation and acquiescence from the beneficiaries on the priorities set by the foundations. The frequent interactions between foundation staff and university administrators, who for the most part handled the grants for their respective departments, provided critical feedback about each institution's perspectives. Through this process and open dialogue, the Partnership foundations received valuable endorsement from universities and academic networks legitimating their role as providers of funds and rightful developers of higher education in Africa.

However, despite this positive dialogue, the Partnership foundations stood on equal footing only among themselves as funders. Akin Aina, program director for Higher Education in Africa at Carnegie, confirms this point:

> The foundations were equal, right from day one, the first four and the three later. You know, not with the universities, not with the African institutes. The foundations were equal among themselves.[3]

This important difference undermines the place of universities and research centers as equal contributors to the agenda for higher education development in Africa, and their actual weight among other contributors such as international donors. In spite of all the efforts to make the voice of Africans heard, the inclusive approach of the PHEA was often tested. Narciso Matos, former program director at Carnegie Corporation of New York, shared this interesting perspective:

> I still recall a vice chancellor of an African university (incidentally he was the vice chancellor of one of the universities that were benefiting financially and otherwise from the partnership) at one of the meeting said 'Is it a partnership of foundations or is it a partnership between foundations and African universities? How are we involved in defining the agenda and so forth?'[4]

The unequal dimension described in these lines reflects a concern that was shared by other grantees who consistently questioned the role they played, and the degree to which they were included in the Partnership's choices. At times, grantors and grantees appeared to carry separate statuses—the foundations were equal among themselves but remained in a category apart from the universities they were meant to serve. Although there was a general consensus among interviewees that the foundations listened to and understood the needs of African universities, the Partnership remained a partnership of foundations rather than a partnership between foundations and universities. Thus, the Partnership foundations always ran the risk of being perceived as dominating the agenda or imposing an American worldview on African universities, as was suggested in a 2004 evaluation of the PHEA: "There are a few critics who feel that the Partnership approach is too rooted in an American worldview of democracy, liberal economics and gender equality as criteria for selecting institutions to support"[5] This point is confirmed by Susan Grant Lewis, the Partnership's coordinator:

> What I had been looking for was a more direct interaction with African scholars and African higher education leaders, and that came to fruition. That was really rewarding: to meet with them, to have conversations, to engage them in two different university leaders' forums. The first one was actually a very frustrating experience because some of the program officers wouldn't let go, and the second one was fantastic because it was organized by a steering committee of African

university leaders, which I staffed. It was much more of a buy-in and the quality
of the whole thing was better, as well.[6]

This passage highlights both the willingness of grantees in the Partnership's
discussions and the complexity this entailed, not to mention the "buy-in" outcome anticipated in this process of inclusion. Nevertheless, there is an obvious
difference between a willingness to hear the grantees' point of view and actually integrating their suggestions to the agenda, as the comment above reflects.
Program officers learned "how to let go." But it was not clear if they were
willing to accept the gradual involvement of grantees in determining funding priorities. Additionally, this sharing process underscores the role of the
Partnership facilitator in creating opportunities for dialogue between grantors
and grantees. It also introduces a connection between legitimation and effective grantmaking, as the inclusion of grantees reflected a practice commonly
accepted as good among the Partnership's program officers and directors.
    It is relevant to examine this issue as both a source of legitimacy for founda-
tions and as strategic leverage for grantees who can level the playing-field by
proposing new areas for funding based on their level of trust with the foundations. This validation is critical for foundations, but also puts grantees in a position of strength relative to the power that the funders hold. This dual exchange
of power and legitimacy was well recognized by the Partnership's actors, most
of whom emphasized having an open dialogue with grantees—as well as a lot
of respect for them—and needing their input, as expressed by Andrea Johnson,
program officer at Carnegie:

> Our agenda, in many respects, came from the universities the foundations were
> working with. Again, IT came directly from that. If you're working with a group
> of universities and all of them are asking as part of their funding to dedicate some
> towards IT, you know IT is a priority. And that to me gives you permission to
> act on that because it's clearly something that's of interest. We did this, in that
> respect, a bottom-up. Not everything was bottom-up, but that was.[7]

Foundations were convinced by universities that information technology was a
priority. This led to a number of important initiatives supported by the foundations, including the creation of the Bandwidth Initiative which provided
cheaper and faster Internet bandwidth to universities on the African continent—a flagship initiative for the PHEA. This initiative did not originate with
the foundations, and was not imposed by anyone. It owes its success to, and is
a resounding evidence of, the foundations' willingness to listen to universities
and fund what universities saw as a priority. Philipp Griffiths, senior advisor at
the Mellon Foundation, commented on the Partnership's philosophy:

> Those designs were done pretty much jointly and frequently in response to
> demand by the recipients so the Partnership is very good about not sort of say-
> ing 'here's a pot of money and we want you to do this with it.' That's not the

way they operate. It's more they sit down with the partner universities and talk through what their priorities are and agree on some course of action.[8]

These types of exchanges between grantors and grantees occurred in early planning stages. The participation of grantees in the PHEA was well established from the very beginning. Indeed, the original Partnership launch in 2000, the re-launch in 2005, and several other public relation events included the presence of university vice-chancellors and individuals from the academic and international education development worlds. Vice-chancellors were well recognized by the Partnership foundations, and several public relations events were organized with their active participation in the form of testimonies, panel discussions, and informal exchanges with international educators in the USA and in Africa.

There was a conscious effort by all those involved in the Partnership to include African perspectives in the Partnership as a safeguard against the power imbalance between foundations and universities. In a Partnership meeting between various program officers about the organization of a University Leaders' Forum, several participants asked whether there were sufficient Africans from Africa to ensure that participants did not feel that they were being talked at. The participation of African institutions in the agenda and development strategies of private funders from the West remains a topic of inexhaustible debate. Although perspectives on the issue of grantee participation in developing the agenda may have varied within the foundations, several comments highlighted that some elements of the agenda were indeed imposed on grantees. The following comment is from Neil Grabois, former vice-president of Carnegie Corporation of New York:

> We did not wish to tell the universities what to do, we wanted to say 'you tell us what you want to do and if we find it a persuasive argument, we'll support you'; except in the case of women's education. We did impose that on them.[9]

The case of women referred to above relates to both women's access to higher education and gender studies programs, and universities' resistance or lack of interest in these types of programs. The ambivalence of this quote highlights the limits of agenda-sharing in the Partnership, and reinforces the unbalanced exchanges that can occur between grantors and grantees. The agenda is set within a mix of grantee-led propositions and pre-established objectives from foundations based on their mission, original focus, and desire to make their mark on a specific issue. An agenda was not necessarily imposed on the grantees; they were invited to submit proposals which needed to fit in the foundations' funding programs. However, the grantees were not involved in establishing these programs' choices, or had minimal input in helping the foundations' establish their strategy. The following comment from David Court confirms this paradigm:

> The weakness of this Partnership is that it didn't involve the clients as formally and openly as it perhaps should have done, and this is something that needs to be done in the future.[10]

In other words, there was a tension between tailoring universities' needs to a foundation's preferred areas of funding, and being able to change a foundation's course with ideas or needs that are relevant to universities or research centers in Africa. It is clear that foundations need to reserve the right to impose certain prerogatives based on their own obligations as organizations governed by deeply institutionalized rules in the USA, such as federal tax laws, or event their charters and bylaws. But one would hope that including grantees in the foundations' agenda at an early enough stage would have the benefit of serving well the foundations' missions and obligations, and confirming their role as drivers of social change.

Although several foundations in the Partnership entrusted African experts with executive responsibilities as directors of their African programs, and although the foundations' beneficiaries were listened to as described earlier with the presence of university vice-chancellors at various Partnership events, the asymmetry of power between grantors and grantees remained significant throughout the duration of the Partnership. To be fair, grantee participation within the Partnership's initiatives was at times on a level playing field, as was the case with the Bandwidth Consortium which put several universities in Africa at the same category as foundations. The prospect of equal partnership, although desired by many, was nevertheless difficult to attain. The following quote from Tade Akin Aina, illustrates this point in sharp terms:

> We have perverted and prostituted the notion of partnership because we have not thought about it in terms of the symmetrical notion of partnership. And we use the notion in a way that has debased it and it is actually an ideological cover for a new form of imperialism (although Americans don't want to hear the word imperialism), a new form of an unequal relationship with non-metropolitan, global south institutions. Foundations know it, and that's also one of the norms of good grantmaking. There is an asymmetry of power when you give money to somebody else.[11]

This thought-provoking quote identifies partnerships as a new mechanism used by grantors to promote a specific worldview and push a preexisting agenda on their beneficiaries in developing countries. It delineates the relationship between grantors and grantees in drastic terms, yet implies that grantors and grantees unwittingly crossed a line in the sand. The quote raises questions with regards to power distribution in the Partnership and how foundations wanted to achieve their goals. While one can disagree with a hegemonic interpretation which views foundations as agencies that impose a post-imperialist agenda on their beneficiaries, there is an obvious asymmetry of power between funder and recipient that limits the possibility of equal partnership. Furthermore, it is revealing that such a view comes from an African scholar hired by a US foundation. It suggests a certain uneasiness which emanates from having to wear two hats and reconcile being both an African scholar and a program director in a large US foundation. It also suggests openness on the part of the foundation which had the vision and the drive to recruit experts from the field as their senior staff, so as to potentially base their funding strategy on more informed choices. The foundations' African program officers and directors provided value-added to the Partnership, sharing their expertise and on-the-ground knowledge with their non-African colleagues. They also provided an opportunity to bridge the gap between grantor and grantee perspectives. This was confirmed by Kole Shettima, director of the John D. and Catherine T. MacArthur Foundation in Nigeria:

> People were very sensitive to the relationship in terms of differences of opinions and differences of how things should be done. Africans who are in the foundations in the headquarters were actively involved... That is where the Africans in the leadership who are involved in the higher education program certainly had their way. They had some leadership role in defining the agenda and what should be done. Certainly there may be some areas where perhaps we could have different opinions but I'm not sure if they were really very different.[12]

Despite several differences in opinion with their colleagues, senior staff from Africa in the Partnership foundations succeeded in infusing the Partnership with an African perspective. This confirms that the Partnership's foundations did not just impose an agenda on Africa's universities, but that they were careful in involving experts and locals in creating an agenda that fitted both parties. Narciso Matos, former program director at Carnegie, commented:

> I was not the only person with previous experience with higher education in Africa. On the other hand I should say I was the only one who came directly from the trenches. I brought to the partnership my previous experience as secretary general of the Association of African Universities. I had been the vice chancellor of an African university which was in many ways emblematic of the kinds of institutions that we wanted to support, and I had the direct experience of teaching and doing research in one of these institutions that we wanted to help develop. So that's what I think I brought to the Partnership.[13]

For many people interviewed, Narciso Matos was the driving force behind the PHEA, at least in its early stage. He brought his experience, notoriety, and connections from past leadership positions in African higher education. He was also a rare exception in the world of foundations as being an African program director at one of the most influential foundations in the world. As a matter of fact, several program officers interviewed hared their uneasiness with having only white people sit at the Partnership's table. The Partnership remained mostly guided by non-Africans, although there were exceptions. Narciso Matos used his unique position at Carnegie to guide the foundation, and the

Partnership's activities closer to what African universities really needed. His presence had an impact on how grantees perceived and accepted the foundations. As a result, Carnegie gained tremendously from putting a former African higher education leader at the helm of its higher education program and in the Partnership's executive committee. Recruiting an African university leader to convey the foundation's agenda to other African university leaders was a bold choice which turned out to have hugely positive impact on the way US foundations worked with universities. It also promoted Carnegie Corporation of New York to a leadership position in the field of higher education development on the African continent. Several foundations had highly competent staff, and those with field offices received input from their local staff. Some of these field officers were also given a leadership role in the Partnership, as Katherine Namuddu from The Rockefeller Foundation Nairobi office who became the foundation's representative to the executive committee of the Partnership. This was a welcome move from Rockefeller, as one would hope to see more local experts rise to executive positions at most international grantmaking organizations. This brings more than just added knowledge and expertise to a funder's strategy. It has the potential of bringing the voice of the beneficiaries closer to the ear of grantmakers.

A key Partnership principle was to respond to priorities identified in consultation with African higher education leaders. Indeed, reports and evaluations confirm that some of the Partnership's actors made real efforts to include several university vice-chancellors and consultants from Africa; the Partnership's actors listened to advice and suggestions from vice-chancellors to identify and address priorities. Kole Shettima commented:

> Definitely, grantees were listened to. There were discussions with them in terms of the future of the partnership, what areas we were likely to support, what new ideas we have. Many of the meetings, they came prepared with their ideas of what they want to see done and we took them seriously in terms of what they want and how it was going to be done.[14]

This quote confirms that there was a respectful exchange between grantors and grantees, and that grantees' views regarding goals and the methods used to reach these goals were heard. However, foundations needed constant reminders so that consultation was not undermined. For instance, several meeting minutes highlighted the role of the University Leaders' Forum which served as a consultative meeting with the PHEA university partners. The foundations were careful about announcing initiatives without undermining consultation with their university partners. It was generally agreed upon that the purposes of the University Leaders' Forum were to advocate for the issue, leverage resources beyond the PHEA, and catalyze action on the ground. To a certain extent, the University Leaders' Forum served not only as a platform for exchange and consultation, but also as a tool to leverage legitimacy for a foundation-led strategy that seemed predetermined. Foundations had to be careful about announcing initiatives, because those initiatives had taken their source in prior programmatic discussions which reinforced the foundations' missions and prerequisites. The Forum among university leaders was used to create a dialogue, discuss potential projects, and hear different perspectives about the future of Africa's higher education. It also served as a legitimation mechanism for foundations that received feedback from university leaders through this conversation.

Participation was also orchestrated through the organization of case studies in order to provide the Partnership with recent research on higher education in Africa. The studies focused on specific higher education systems (Ghana, Tanzania, Mozambique, Kenya, and South Africa) or universities (Makerere).[15] The objective of the case studies was to improve the foundations' understanding of institutional change through exchanges of experience. This would draw attention to specific experiences, internal factors, and external content. The defined purpose of the case studies was therefore to advance understanding of the process of institutional and systemic change, focusing on institutional innovations within their national contexts. The case studies' objective was to guide the Partnership's funding strategy and base it on solid grounds. Each case study focused on a specific Partnership country, so as to determine the needs of universities in their respective environment, and direct resources and programs to better serve them.

> Differently from what has been done in the past, where you would select a consultant and have him or her write a study, the development of this study was done directly by African scholars. It was very interactive. All the countries that were selected to be part of the partnership were invited to a series of workshops where they would visit the findings of the studies' authors, they would make comments in a manner that not only enriched each individuals study but made each study better than the previous one.[16]

The collaboration between grantors and grantees was set on an equal footing and produced positive results. The case studies served as participatory mechanisms to build a common agenda for higher education development in the Partnership's target countries. They also helped identify key participants on the ground. There was a clear desire to build the PHEA's strategy on data and good research, rather than have it driven by the foundations or national governments. The case studies were first and foremost meant to involve university leaders in a consultation with the Partnership's foundations. The foundations consulted vice-chancellors from various universities on the choice of internal case study writers, who were often individuals with a high stature within the academic institutions.

It is important to note that in most African higher education systems, vice-chancellors are university presidents nominated by the respective governments. Thus, the foundations also fought hard to avoid politicizing the case studies, particularly when approaching complex higher education systems such as in South Africa and Nigeria. All recognized the need for governments to buy into the study findings, particularly the portion of the studies that focused on the higher education system in each country, but concerns were raised over how to do this without over-politicizing the study. Indeed, foundations intended to use the cases studies to convince governments and university leaders, and as such to validate the foundations' plan of action based on the findings of the case studies. However, the validity and usefulness of the case studies were questioned. They served as a process for establishing a dialogue with African universities and developing a grantmaking strategy that was more suited to their needs and cultural particularities. Indeed, the placement of the foundations in the US provided some physical and philosophical distance from African universities and stakeholders, as well as a degree of detachment from special interests—a fact which was well known by the Partnership participants. But the case studies were not unanimously seen as an adequate tool for solving issues and instigating reforms. The foundations debated their efficacy and depth, among other issues. The case studies were not seen as a good way of studying thematic issues. For a number of people interviewed, the case studies were too superficial; they did not deal adequately with the financing of higher education, or gender studies. Innovations and transformations were not clearly defined or did not lead to institutional reform. Although they became a valuable contribution to the literature on African higher education, the case studies were ultimately given less weight in the foundations' grantmaking strategy. However, the Partnership's evaluation reports indicated that the case studies were an important tangible product of the Partnership. They were distributed in hard copy widely to libraries in Africa and to African research organizations, as well as to scores of university vice-chancellors across Africa. As such, the case studies helped the Partnership's foundations establish themselves as a new collaborative force. They disseminated the Partnership's vision for African higher education via the endorsement of the vice-chancellors and researchers who participated in their making.

In *Actors and System* (1980), Michel Crozier posited that one should take into consideration the conflicting strategies of actors; their "human construct," particularly when they engage in collective action and pursue contradictory interests:

> When results of collective action are the opposite of what individual actors wished, it is never merely because of the prosperities of the problem. It is always also the result of the human structuration of the field of action, that is, because of the characteristics of the organization or of the system in which the actors interact and to which they are committed.[17]

According to Crozier, rational individuals place their own interests above those of others, and as such bargain with or manipulate others ideologically or affectively. The Partnership's aggregation of individual perspectives reveals a bargaining, if not manipulative, quality in the discourse of philanthropic foundations in African higher education. This discourse and its participants contributed to legitimizing the foundations' work in higher education in Africa.

These individuals nonetheless negotiated between the collective interests of the Partnership, those of their respective institution, and their own interests as professionals in their fields.

Governance in the Partnership's grantor–grantee relationship was not truly consultative despite considerable efforts on the part of program officers and directors in the partner foundations. Africans participated, but not as the driving force. Legitimacy was a resource provided by grantees, who, for this reason, needed to be invited to the table and asked to participate in the agenda. The asymmetry of power remained throughout the Partnership's 10-year existence, but the partner foundations also acknowledged that more grantee consultation and participation was necessary. Foundations were attributed legitimacy not because of what they did or how they did it, but through a bargaining process. The Partnership received endorsement from its grantees who, by being involved at varying degrees in the Partnership's processes, provided a form of approval and validation which was both sought after and orchestrated by the grantors. This type of validation of practices and procedures resulted in normalizing legitimacy.

Issues regarding the universities' dependency on donor funding have remained, particularly with respect to unequal partnerships between richly endowed foundations in the USA and institutions in the global south seeking resources. This is especially important in the case of foundations interacting with universities in Africa. These relationships were nurtured in a context of scarce resources for research agendas that did not always match those of the grantors, but were modified for the sake of accessing available funds. In addition, there was competition for resources among recipient institutions at the same time that these institutions were putting pressure on national governments to be more responsive to their needs. This debate, however, goes beyond the simple role of foundations in developing countries or on their influence on universities in Africa. The discussion encompasses all types of non-African international donors, development agencies, and philanthropic organizations that seek to play a role in the development of Africa, particularly when these donors set priorities and strategies with limited participation from Africans.

NOTES

1. See for instance "Donor Collaboration: Power in Number" by the Philanthropic Initiative (2010).
2. August 10, 2011 interview with Andrea Johnson, program officer of the Carnegie Corporation of New York.
3. September 26, 2011 interview in New York with Tade Akin Aina, program director for the Carnegie Corporation of New York.
4. September 9, 2011 phone interview with Narciso Matos, former program director for the Carnegie Corporation of New York.
5. Moja et al. (2004), p. 20.
6. July 8, 2011 phone interview with Susan Grant Lewis, coordinator of the Partnership for Higher Education in Africa.

7. August 10, 2011 interview in New York with Andrea Johnson, program officer for the Carnegie Corporation of New York.
8. July 20, 2011 phone interview with Phillip Griffiths, advisor for The Andrew W. Mellon Foundation.
9. August 19, 2011 interview in New York with Neil Grabois, former vice-president for the Carnegie Corporation of New York.
10. September 29, 2011 phone interview with David Court, former program officer for The Rockefeller Foundation.
11. September 26, 2011 interview in New York with Tade Akin Aina, program director for the Carnegie Corporation of New York.
12. June 22, 2011 phone interview with Kole Shettima, program director for the John D. and Catherine T. MacArthur Foundation.
13. September 9, 2011 phone interview with Narciso Matos, former program director, Carnegie Corporation of New York.
14. June 22, 2011 phone interview with Kole Shettima, program director, The John D. and Catherine T. MacArthur Foundation.
15. The PHEA studies included:

   – Manuh et al. (2007) Change & Transformation in Ghana's Publicly Funded Universities.
   – Mkude et al. (2003) Higher Education in Tanzania.
   – Musisi and Muwanga (2003) Makerere University in Transition 1993–2000. Opportunities & Challenges.
   – Mário et al. (2003) Higher Education in Mozambique.
   – Cloete et al. (2004) National Policy & a Regional Response in South African Higher Education.
   – Mwiria et al. (2007) Public & Private Universities in—Kenya. New Challenges, Issues & Achievements.
   – Pereira (2007) Gender in the Making of the Nigerian University System.

16. September 9, 2011 phone interview with Narciso Matos, former program director, Carnegie Corporation of New York.
17. Crozier (1980), p. 4.

BIBLIOGRAPHY

Cloete, N., P. Pillay, S. Badat, and T. Moja. 2004. *National policy and a regional response in South African higher education*. Oxford: James Curry.
Crozier, Michel. 1980. *Actors and system*. Chicago: The University of Chicago Press.
Frumkin, Peter. 2006. *Strategic giving: The art and science of philanthropy*. Chicago: University of Chicago Press.
Manuh, Takyiwaa, Sulley Gariba, and Joseph Budu. 2007. *Change & transformation in Ghana's publicly funded universities. A study of experiences, lessons & opportunities*. Accra: Woeli Publishing Services.
Mário, Mouzinho, Peter Fry, Lisbeth Levey, and Arlindo Chilundo. 2003. *Higher education in Mozambique. A case study*. Maputo: Imprensa & Livraria Universitaria, Universidade Eduardo Mondlane.

Mkude, Daniel, Brian Cooksey, and Lisbeth Levey. 2003. *Higher education in Tanzania. A case study.* Dar es Salaam: Mkuki na Nyota.

Moja T., J. Reddy, and A. White. (2004). *Evaluation of the Partnership for Higher Education in Africa.* Unpublished.

Musisi, Nakanyike B., and Nansozi K. Muwanga. 2003. *Makerere University in transition 1993–2000. Opportunities & challenges.* Kampala: Fountain Publishers.

Mwiria, Kilemi, Njuguna Ng'ethe, Charles Ngome, Douglas Ouma-Odero, Violet Wawire, and Daniel Wesonga. 2007. *Public & private universities in Kenya. New challenges, issues & achievements.* Nairobi: East African Educational Publishers.

Pereira, Charmaine. 2007. *Gender in the making of the Nigerian University System.* Ibadan: Heinemann Educational Books.

Philanthropic Initiative. (2015). Donor collaboration: Power in numbers. Boston, MA.

CHAPTER 10

Conclusion: Equal Participation and the Challenges of Higher Education Philanthropy

The discussion in the preceding chapters encompassed the specifics of high-impact grantmaking among leading US foundations, with a particular focus on several trend-setting foundations in the field of higher education in Africa: Carnegie Corporation of New York, Ford Foundation, John D. and Catherine T. MacArthur Foundation, The Rockefeller Foundation, The William and Flora Hewlett Foundation, The Andrew W. Mellon Foundation, and The Kresge Foundation. The considerable impact of these foundations over African higher education, accumulated over decades of strategic grantmaking in the field, remains unrivaled. Their vast influence is truly remarkable considering the relatively small size of their investments to academic institutions. These foundations, demonstrating a high level of expertise in the field, maximized their investments, impact, influence, and legitimacy, particularly in relation to institutions of higher learning in Africa. The research presented in this book focused on the role of institutional, inter-organizational, and environmental factors in the relationship between US foundations and higher education institutions in Africa. The findings help to explain the dynamics of collaboration in the PHEA, as well as the ways in which collaboration served the foundations involved. These dynamics of collaboration framed the discourse of philanthropic foundations and the extent to which collaborative mechanisms increase the complexity of grantor–grantee relations.

Grantees must compete for grants, and although their research agendas do not always match those of donors, their priorities are realigned in order to access the available funds. In addition, competition for resources among recipient institutions complicates collaborative efforts that could change a country's education system. Foundations must also resist pressure from national governments to be responsive to economic and development priorities. Donor-initiated reforms must face the grantees' resistance to change inherited from years of institutional upheavals, and ownership claims emanating from university-led autonomy-oriented policies.

© The Editor(s) (if applicable) and The Author(s) 2016
F. Jaumont, *Unequal Partners*, Philanthropy and Education,
DOI 10.1057/978-1-137-59348-1_10

US foundations have positioned themselves strategically as key stakeholders in African higher education. Furthermore, foundations also produce positive results in the education systems of recipient countries. The Partnership's foundations supported African universities in multiple ways, first, by listening to their grantees' perspectives and establishing participatory mechanisms, and second, by focusing on institutional development and capacity building. Through this process, and the collaboration that they formed the foundations generated valuable impact on the field of higher education in Africa while leveraging more funds and directly contributing to the development of important sectors such as information technology and Internet bandwidth for all universities on the continent. Much to their credit, the foundations' investments supported many research initiatives across the African continent and strengthened pan-African organizations, as well as the next generation of academics.

The relationship and interaction between donors, particularly Partnership participants, was complex. Issues related to interpersonal tensions, hierarchical constraints, changes in leadership and grantee participation had a significant impact on organizational efficiency. Collaboration between the Partnership's foundations encountered a strong degree of resistance because of individualistic tendencies that were embedded in each foundation and their representatives. Indeed, private foundations with distinct missions, processes, and even opposite understanding of development do not converge nor even coexist easily. However, the Partnership foundations reflected shared interests and affinities that superseded these differences, despite the fact that they were established in different socio-cultural eras. As such, the Partnership served as a vehicle that pushed the foundations toward collaboration, rather than simply following their natural inclination toward independent grantmaking. This was in part made possible because each foundation accepted the fact that not one foundation could act alone to solve issues as complex as those presented to them by African universities. Program officers navigated the various obstacles and constraints that are implied by such a large collaboration. Nonetheless, the preference in each foundation for individual action remains, and one can only hope that more and more foundations accept the principles of collaboration and make the necessary compromises implied in working collaboratively to generate greater impact in the future. The Partnership foundations were pioneers on this front, surmounting the collaboration's organizational challenges through constant rationalization and negotiation among themselves. In doing so, the participants constantly gained and learned from each other. In the end, adapting the organizational imperatives of each foundation to the operational modalities of the Partnership generated positive results, not only in the aggregation of funds toward joint targets, but also in the transfer of knowledge among grantmakers who could venture in unchartered funding territory while reducing some of the risks. These advantages maximized the impact of foundations on the field of higher education in Africa. As developers, their collective prestige and power allowed them to reach new scale by serving more universities, research centers, and academic networks than could have been served otherwise. The aggregated efforts of the foundations resulted in raising awareness about the field of higher education as a whole which had been neglected for decades.

Universities have now become the focus of international donors and national governments. The pressure for greater outcomes and accountability among Partnership members, which necessitated the addition of new collaborative processes, contributed to this change. As a result of their collaboration, Partnership foundations have improved the way universities are now perceived and aided. As such, universities have gained respectability by becoming active participants in Africa's future. The foundations succeeded in reinforcing an agenda which promoted a discourse of capacity building and institutional development. In doing so, they encouraged university administrators to establish new financial and managerial initiatives, while improving infrastructures and information technology and supporting new fields of inquiry and training programs that fitted the economic needs of their target countries. This strategy was designed by the foundations through a process of participation and consultation with their beneficiaries, who contributed to the conversation and validated the foundations' actions. This process was also internal to the foundations as it included experts and evaluators, many from Africa, who assessed the foundations' strategies in terms of their capacity to generate appropriate and desirable changes in African higher education.

The PHEA was the sum of all the individuals that composed it. These individuals negotiated the collective interests of the Partnership and those of their respective institutions, while upholding their own particular interpretation of social change. While it was clear that the partners were primarily concerned with the necessary structural and procedural obligations to make the collaboration work, they did their best to respond to the specific needs and challenges faced by their grantees. By including grantees in the Partnership's decision-making process and capitalizing on the weight of foundation leaders on the foundations' assets and strategy, the PHEA was able to make the foundations' work more relevant to the needs of higher education institutions in Africa. The authority of foundation leaders had an obvious impact on the Partnership's intra and extra-organizational equilibrium, particularly as the Partnership was initiated by the presidents themselves. When the PHEA was launched, the presidents of Carnegie Corporation of New York, John D. and Catherine T. MacArthur Foundation, The Rockefeller Foundation, and Ford Foundation, sought to deliver a strong message regarding the importance of higher education in Africa. In this sense, foundation leaders did not only instigate the Partnership's vision but also leaned on their authority to legitimize their vision. The presidents of each foundation exercised substantial influence on the collaboration, on program priorities, on power distribution, and on the delegation of duties. By being involved in varying degrees in the Partnership's processes, grantees provided a form of approval and validation, and in return, the Partnership received endorsement from grantees. This was both sought after and orchestrated by the grantors. This type of validation was necessary to obtain some legitimacy for the initiatives undertaken. Grantee endorsement, however, occurred within the context of power asymmetry.

The unequal nature of the Partnership was sometimes a concern for grantees who always questioned their role and share of participation. Grantors and grantees carried separate statuses; the foundations were equal among themselves but not with the universities they purported to serve. This difference of status had a bearing on how the agenda was defined. Although there was a general consensus among the participants and the study's interviewees that the foundations had heard and understood the needs of African universities, the Partnership remained a partnership of foundations, as opposed to a partnership of foundations and universities, as several foundation staff indicated. Thus, running the risk of being perceived as dominating the agenda or imposing an American worldview on African universities was always a concern. The question of grantee participation, and the tension that it produced on both sides of the grantor–grantee relationship, created a context for legitimacy normalization. This, in turn, had a positive impact on the grantor–grantee relationship and on the foundations' grantmaking overall. This issue was both a positive source of legitimacy for foundations and a guarantee for grantees to level the playing-field with grantors. Such validation was substantial for foundations and also put grantees in a stronger position. This point was well recognized by the Partnership's actors, most of whom claimed to have significantly considered grantee perspectives in their choices. To surmount the hurdles of power asymmetry, foundations insisted that grantee consultation and participation were important criteria for good grantmaking decisions.

The close relationship between foundations and select universities in Africa suggests not only that both institutions have influenced each other for a long period of time, but also that they have established a competitive field which puts pressure on weaker institutions. Without other competing financial contributors or governmental constraints, the foundations were effective in asserting their leadership in the field of higher education, particularly in former British colonies. The Partnership foundations established connections and acquired access to the best organizations of higher learning in Africa as well as to new generations of academics and students, particularly in institutions which used English as their primary language of instruction. The foundations also positioned themselves strategically in the ecology of international developers to advocate for the importance of higher education in the development of Africa. They did so while promoting their conception of knowledge societies throughout current or former Commonwealth countries on the continent. By expanding their scope and expertise to higher education in Africa, the Partnership's foundations asserted their role as higher education developers as they provided support to select universities, research centers, and scholastic networks. In return, these influential beneficiaries reinforced the legitimacy and accountability of the foundations by accepting their grants and agenda. At the same time, these foundations maintained an agenda close to their own worldview of democracy, liberal economics and gender equality.

UNEQUAL PARTNERS, DEPENDENCY, AND THE DISCOURSE ON PRIORITIES

Issues regarding the dependency of universities on donor funding have remained, particularly with respect to unequal partnerships between richly endowed foundations in the USA and resource-seeking institutions in the global south. This is especially important in the case of foundations interacting with universities in Africa. This debate, however, goes beyond the simple role of foundations in developing countries or on their influence on universities in Africa. The discussion encompasses all types of non-African international donors, development agencies, and philanthropic organizations that seek to play a role in the development of Africa, particularly when these donors set priorities and strategies with limited participation from Africans. Many significant questions arise from this debate, and future research should examine whether US foundations can embrace Africa's development on Africa's terms, and if African universities can gain full ownership over their participation in US foundations developing strategies for Africa.

Much to their credit, the investments of the foundations led to the successful support of research initiatives across a number of institutions. The Partnership also contributed to the strengthening of pan-African academic organizations such as the Association of African Universities and the Council for the Development of Social Science Research. Other areas of focus and massive investment included information technology and the provision of Internet bandwidth at affordable prices for African universities. Stepping outside their comfort zone, the Partnership's foundations tackled the issue of internet accessibility which their grantees viewed as a priority. In this manner, the foundations found an opportunity to use their collective weight and influence to generate change on a wide scale. Developing bandwidth and reducing Internet access costs for universities were not traditional foundation initiatives. Nevertheless, the foundations succeeded in leveraging economies of scale by forming a consortium of universities which purchased Internet bandwidth in bulk, thus achieving volume discounts and extending their savings to higher education and research institutions in Africa. The extent to which Partnership foundations contributed to the structure and institutionalization of the field of higher education in Africa can be observed through their success in reinforcing increasingly prestigious universities throughout the continent. However, institutionalizing the field of African higher education did not imply controlling the agenda for higher education in Africa, as the aggregate power of foundations was far too small to have any large-scale impact on a continent. The Partnership foundations relied on the multiplying effect of their focus on the development of universities in Africa which they selected for having already engaged in the process of modernization. This strategic approach remains questionable, as one could argue that a foundation's impact would be far greater if it focused on a larger group of weaker institutions. Of some 800 universities in Africa, less than 10 % receive support from US foundations, leaving too many institutions out of the race.

Furthermore, considering the importance of language and culture in the mechanisms of globalization, and acknowledging that language groups compete in the knowledge economy, the influence of US foundations in Africa reinforced the dominance of English as the lingua franca of the continent's development. By favoring higher education organizations that use English as the language of internal and external communication and learning, US foundations created durable connections with the continent's future leaders and entrepreneurs. Universities in Francophone, Lusophone, and Arabophone countries appear to be less equipped for receiving grants from US foundations. Both foundations and universities in these countries should reach out to each other and work together to remedy this problem. The geopolitical agenda of the Partnership might not have been formulated with specific postcolonial considerations. Nonetheless, colonial lines emerge as clear demarcations between Africa's new knowledge societies. These lines are reinforced by US foundations' grantmaking strategies in institutions that use English as the dominant language. However, the Partnership foundations succeeded in raising the profile of higher education on the entire continent. However, they concentrated their efforts on a select number of institutions; the approach of the Partnership foundations has become an example for others to follow. Thus, the foundations have succeeded in influencing the ecology of donors—such as government budgets, international organizations, and development agencies. The World Bank and other international donors such as foreign development agencies, European foundations, pan-African development funds and other US foundations have praised the work of the PHEA. Their priorities have shifted, and now give more importance to universities and their quest for institutional sustainability and resources. The discourse on priorities in African higher education is placed in a contested terrain, where grantors and grantees not only negotiate varied logistical perspectives but also compete within inhospitable national contexts. In certain African countries, governments do not necessarily encourage the development of universities or international donors who are not overtly cooperative. The Partnership foundations gained legitimacy by helping universities become self-sustainable and less dependent on external funding. They did so by raising awareness and making the case for universities in national contexts. However, the Partnership foundations did not engage sufficiently with national governments, even when this was important to generate more sustainability for universities and reduce dependency on foreign donors.

General Reflections

Many international donors value capacity building as the key focus of their funding strategy. To a more figurative extent, capacity building functions as a ceremonial rite that frames the conversation of higher education development. This rite rallies donors around a common philosophy of development, a jargon, and a method which focuses primarily on the infrastructure, human resource, and financial mechanisms of one's grant recipient, and encourages its development and institutionalization. Thus, capacity building is not just today's buzz word; it serves as a unifying principle that draws together grantors and grantees. The rhetoric of institutionalization was prevalent among the PHEA, as it helped the foundations conform to the myths and the ceremonial rite of capacity building by becoming the collaboration's primary objective. This does not mean that the Partnership was a purely rhetorical exercise. Member foundations did, however, share a certain language—a key set of terms framing the Partnership's objectives and a way of telling the story that found its source in the dominant myth of the moment across the ecology of international donors. If one needed to conform and adhere to the myth and rituals of capacity building in order to belong to one's institutional environment, speaking the language of higher education developers and of international development in general, appears to have been an essential trait of the grantmakers referenced thus far. Capacity building is also a transformative mechanism that can legitimize the actions of funders. It adds to one's credibility, and procures more legitimacy to one's action. Ultimately, the best players gain more influence on the field that they seek to transform, while opening the possibility of setting new trends.

The Partnership foundations focus extensively on institutional development and capacity building. This was not only part of the individual strategies of the foundations; it reflected their adherence to the myth and its rites, while reinforcing affinity among the partners. As an approach that conformed to the codes of international donors, capacity building helped the foundations leverage credibility, funding, and legitimacy among the funders. It also worked as useful rhetoric to unify the mission, vision, and strategy of the foundations in the Partnership. While foundations conformed to the myth of capacity building, they also advocated for universities as institutions that deserved more attention from international donors. The foundations unfolded their strategy around the modernization of libraries and research centers, Internet bandwidth on campuses, fundraising and leadership seminars, governance development, higher education studies, strategic plans, and consultancy. Similar to their actions in the realm of US higher education, foundations as a whole appeared content to meet the core capacity and capital needs of African universities, rather than pushing these institutions to change and prepare themselves for major access issues confronting the field. The rhetoric of capacity building conferred more legitimacy upon the foundations. The myth of capacity building and the ceremonial act of impact investing gave foundations enough justification and collective endorsement to eventually maximize legitimacy.

Furthermore, the Partnership's foundations tended to resist isomorphism and standardization in order to maintain their institutional differences and particular vantage points. Collaboration and convergence were used as accessories to the foundations' strategies of legitimation. This was clearly the case with capacity building which functioned as a unifying, rationalized myth to which foundations adhered and aligned. Yet, this myth was transformed and used as a justification, as opposed to an effective mechanism, by the foundations. The Partnership's strategic alignment exemplifies this point. Isomorphism was resisted and collaboration negotiated, resulting in the use of a rationalized myth to justify one's role, and hide mishaps and ineffective actions. As such, the myth of capacity building should be sublimated by another rationalized myth which could strengthen the relationship between grantors and grantees. An officially proclaimed principle central to the Partnership was to respond to priorities identified through consultation with African higher education leaders. Indeed, reports and evaluations confirm that some of the Partnership's actors made real efforts to include several university vice-chancellors and consultants from Africa; the Partnership's actors listened to advice and suggestions from vice-chancellors to identify and address priorities. There was a respectful exchange between grantors and grantees, and the views of grantees regarding goals and the methods suggested to reach these goals were heard. However, the Partnership foundations could have generated more positive change by including faculty, researchers, and even students in consultation processes that defined their grantmaking strategies. This form of consultative participation would reinforce foundations in their role as pioneers and risk-takers while supporting social change and addressing issues that are meaningful to individuals on the ground. In actuality, foundation representatives needed constant reminders of the importance of consultation so that grantees were not undermined and power dynamics did not mold the relationship. Furthermore, grantee participation was a source of legitimation and not of equalization, as the asymmetry of power remained active. In this sense, governance in the Partnership's grantor–grantee relationship was top down rather than truly consultative. Africans participated but were not the driving force: they were invited to the table and asked to participate in the agenda because they provided the resource of legitimacy. Foundations were attributed legitimacy not because of what they did or how they did it, but through a bargaining process.

The relative power of the presidents had significant bearing on normalizing legitimacy in the eyes of the Partnership participants. Indeed, having their support meant that the time spent by program officers on collaboration was valued within the foundation; officers were given funding to make the work of collaboration worthwhile and potentially effective. In the case of the Partnership, the channels of legitimacy disappeared when the replacement of presidents signaled the demise of the collaboration. Governance in the case of the Partnership did not solely rest on the charisma of the foundations' presidents but on normalizing legitimacy obtained through interpersonal exchanges at all levels. The omnipotence of foundation presidents in the decision-making and their implicit legitimation role meant that foundation staff had to manoeuver within constraints set by their leaders. They were ultimately accountable to the presidents. In this sense, the concentration of power in the hands of foundation leaders is an important aspect of understanding internal accountability and legitimation mechanisms in US foundations. The foundations' African program officers and directors provided value to the Partnership, sharing their expertise and local knowledge with their non-African colleagues. They also provided an opportunity to bridge the gap between grantor and grantee perspectives. But, this expertise was intensely negotiated with the power held by the presidents and was limited by the constraints of the foundations' hierarchical structures.

The nature of power in inter-organizational relationships led grantees to believe that acting in the interests of more powerful partners was consistent with their own interests. Yet, those interests were still molded by the power dynamic. Nevertheless, the Partnership received endorsement from its grantees, who by being involved in varying degrees in the Partnership's processes, provided a form of approval and validation that was both sought after and orchestrated by the grantors. As such, the power asymmetry appears to have been remodeled to some degree, as the value of grantee endorsement increased. However, this exchange placed the Partnership's foundations and the African universities that they funded on an equal footing. With their status as organizations that serve the common good, foundations are validated through their inclusion in a category of organizations perceived as pursuing communally valuable goals. This is different from perceptions based on specific results achieved. The Partnership's foundations capitalized on the legitimacy accorded to the non-profit and voluntary sector in order to emphasize the significance and precedence of higher education in the economic development of Africa. Among higher education developers, legitimacy is both essential to one's actions and a malleable resource that can be shaped or co-opted. Indeed, collaborative and environmental factors contributed to legitimizing the role and goals of the foundations in higher education in Africa. The advocacy component of the Partnership—in the eyes of their constituents, provided legitimacy to the foundations as they strove to achieve policy outcomes, reflecting a general commitment to environmental principles and practices valued by grantees.

Within the discourse of neo-institutionalism and resource dependency, US foundations clearly emerge as non-material entities that are shaped by values, norms, and ideas embedded in their institutional context at home. Yet, these values are epitomized, transformed, and disseminated by foundations' leaders before being internalized by program officers. The latter conform to existing rules and values in order to legitimize their role and action, as they are bound by their hierarchical environment. Program officers adjust their behavior to existing institutional frameworks, which are delineated by the authority of their leaders. The force of this authority is exemplified by individual actions, on the results of collective decisions, and on the quality of coexistence with other institutions. While other constraints may interfere, this authority still has a significant bearing on the foundation's relationships with other institutions. Thus, foundations do not necessarily embody the societal situation prevailing at the time of their inception, as neo-institutionalists posit. Instead, they embody the charismatic authority of their omnipotent leaders, which fluctuates and is modified during each leadership change.

Since foundations use co-optive strategies to gain legitimacy from African universities, universities possess the ability to negotiate their position within the constraints imposed by the preconceived agendas of the foundations. Thus, the partnership between US foundations and African universities could be seen as functioning in a continuous circle of serving and being served. This highlights a rationalized myth that provides legitimacy to grantors and ownership to grantees. In this sense, external resource dependence affects both resource providers and resource seekers. African universities would act strategically to manage their resource dependencies while foundations would act strategically to manage their legitimacy. The dynamic interaction and evolution of universities in relation to foundations could be redefined according to this new myth of equal participation. Hence, internal and trans-organizational dynamics were maneuvered to the advantage of both universities and foundations by including a participatory mechanism that struck the right balance between equal ownership and legitimacy.

In order to bring change to higher education in Africa, the Partnership's foundations needed legitimacy. Thus, they carefully monitored the various legitimation mechanisms of their collaboration while safe-guarding their respective agendas. The dynamics of their collaboration with African universities remained characterized by an unequal relationship. By expanding their scope and expertise to higher education in developing countries, foundations have asserted their role in the building of knowledge societies on a global scale, providing support to academic institutions, research centers, and scholastic networks. They have also pushed the boundaries of their legitimacy and accountability by extending their philanthropic activities and their own views of knowledge production to the rest of the world.

The complex relationship between donors and grantees developed in the context of scarce resources. At times, grantees' research agendas were modified for the sake of access to available funds when they did not match those of the grantors. Competition for resources among recipient institutions complicated collaborative efforts to change the education system. Collaboration must also resist pressure from national governments to be responsive to economic and development priorities. Donor-initiated reforms must face the grantees' resistance to change inherited from years of institutional upheavals. Yet, foundations have stimulated interest in collaborative projects and in the generation of data on higher education in Africa that will be sustained without dependency on donor funding.

Much to their credit, the investments of the Partnership foundations supported many research initiatives across the African continent and strengthened pan-African organizations. Other areas of focus included information technology, with massive investment in Internet bandwidth at affordable prices to African universities. The Partnership foundations attempted to re-energize and empower African higher education networks and academic institutions the success of which has yet to be measured. Foundations were also in a position to propose new policy and reforms to a number of institutions. As a result, the foundations' influence over a small elite group of African universities may drive a divisive wedge within university systems or perhaps fore institutions to enter a competitive race for which they might not be equipped to handle.

Today, African universities are re-emerging as critical engines for economic, social, and development growth in Africa. They represent a primary locus for Western innovation and provide considerable influence over the continent's future leaders in both the public and private sectors. In addition, universities offer African women unprecedented access to education and opportunity, expanding the pool of African experts who will contribute to the continent's efforts to reduce poverty, among other crucial challenges. Questions about the degree of grantee participation in the foundations' preconceived agenda remain. It will take more effort from US foundations to nurture institutional agency in local organizations, and to reinforce the role of African universities in the early stages of their decision-making processes and development strategies.

Appendix A

Table A.1 List of interviewees

Name	Affiliation	Title
Gara LaMarche	Atlantic Philanthropies	Former President
Andrea Johnson	Carnegie Corporation of New York	Program Officer, African Higher Education
Narciso Matos	Carnegie Corporation of New York	Former Director, Higher Education and Libraries in Africa
Patricia Rosenfield	Carnegie Corporation of New York	Director of National Program
Tade Akin Aina	Carnegie Corporation of New York	Director, Higher Education and Libraries in Africa
Claudia Fritelli	Carnegie Corporation of New York	Program Officer, Higher Education and Libraries in Africa
Neil Grabois	Carnegie Corporation of New York	Former Vice-President
Megan Lindow	Chronicle of Higher Education	US Reporter in South Africa
Dina El'Khawaga	Ford Foundation	Program Officer, Cairo Office
Janice Petrovich	Ford Foundation	Former Program Director
John Butler-Adam	Ford Foundation	Program Officer, South Africa Office
Jonathan Friedman	Partnership for Higher Education in Africa	Project Associate
Sue Grant Lewis	Partnership for Higher Education in Africa	Coordinator
Phillip Griffith	The Andrew Mellon Foundation	Senior Advisor
Stuart Saunders	The Andrew Mellon Foundation	Senior Advisor
Raul Davion	The John & Catherine MacArthur Foundation	Director, Higher Education Initiative in Africa
Kole Shettima	The John & Catherine MacArthur Foundation	Director, Nigeria Office
William Moses	The Kresge Foundation	Senior Program Officer
David Court	The Rockefeller Foundation	Former Director, Nairobi Office
Joyce Moock	The Rockefeller Foundation	Former Associate Vice President
Tamara Fox	The William & Flora Hewlett Foundation	Former Program Officer, Population Program

© The Editor(s) (if applicable) and The Author(s) 2016
F. Jaumont, *Unequal Partners*, Philanthropy and Education,
DOI 10.1057/978-1-137-59348-1

Appendix B

Table A.2 Top 25 US foundations in total amount of grants to Africa

Rank	Name	Grant total	Notes
1	Bill & Melinda Gates Foundation	$1,393,085,881	
2	Ford Foundation	$521,901,240	PHEA
3	The Rockefeller Foundation	$304,231,884	PHEA
4	The Atlantic Philanthropies	$224,151,816	
5	Carnegie Corporation of New York	$173,031,220	PHEA
6	W.K. Kellogg Foundation	$172,372,583	
7	The John D. and Catherine T. MacArthur Foundation	$119,412,567	PHEA
8	The Andrew W. Mellon Foundation	$99,732,440	PHEA
9	The William and Flora Hewlett Foundation	$86,930,468	PHEA
10	The Coca-Cola Foundation, Inc.	$71,064,830	
11	Foundation to Promote Open Society	$61,009,972	
12	The David and Lucile Packard Foundation	$58,013,838	
13	A Glimmer of Hope Foundation	$54,119,011	
14	Charles Stewart Mott Foundation	$50,939,261	
15	Howard G. Buffett Foundation	$31,597,204	
16	The McKnight Foundation	$29,721,588	
17	The Bristol-Myers Squibb Foundation, Inc.	$29,453,610	
18	The Kresge Foundation	$29,147,325	PHEA
19	Open Society Institute	$25,871,774	
20	Tides Foundation	$24,494,103	
21	UN Women's Fund for Gender Equality	$24,394,255	
22	Open Doors International, Inc.	$23,565,460	
23	American Jewish World Service	$21,876,986	
24	Firelight Endowment	$15,298,738	
25	Koch Foundation, Inc.	$13,876,314	

Grants made between 2003 and 2013 (Source: Foundation Center)

© The Editor(s) (if applicable) and The Author(s) 2016
F. Jaumont, *Unequal Partners*, Philanthropy and Education,
DOI 10.1057/978-1-137-59348-1

APPENDIX C

Table A.3 Top 40 US foundations in number of grants to Africa

Rank	Name	Number of grants	Notes
1	Ford Foundation	2209	PHEA
2	Firelight Endowment	1089	
3	Koch Foundation, Inc.	943	
4	American Jewish World Service	613	
5	The Global Fund for Women	612	
6	The Rockefeller Foundation	599	PHEA
7	Tides Foundation	491	
8	Charles Stewart Mott Foundation	466	
9	Fund For Global Human Rights, Inc.	403	
10	The Bristol-Myers Squibb Foundation, Inc.	367	
11	Bill & Melinda Gates Foundation	338	
12	Global Fund for Children	328	
13	The John D. and Catherine T. MacArthur Foundation	306	PHEA
14	W.K. Kellogg Foundation	300	
15	The Andrew W. Mellon Foundation	274	PHEA
16	The McKnight Foundation	247	
17	Raskob Foundation for Catholic Activities, Inc.	245	
18	The Atlantic Philanthropies	210	
19	Carnegie Corporation of New York	189	PHEA
20	National Endowment for Democracy	183	
21	Rockefeller Brothers Fund, Inc.	166	
22	The William and Flora Hewlett Foundation	147	PHEA
23	Open Society Institute	142	
24	New Field Foundation	134	
25	Disability Rights Fund	119	
26	The David and Lucile Packard Foundation	117	
27	Banyan Tree Foundation	115	
28	Global Greengrants Fund	93	
29	The Michael and Susan Dell Foundation	90	
30	King Baudouin Foundation United States, Inc.	82	
31	The Christensen Fund	75	

(continued)

© The Editor(s) (if applicable) and The Author(s) 2016
F. Jaumont, *Unequal Partners*, Philanthropy and Education,
DOI 10.1057/978-1-137-59348-1

Table A.3 (continued)

Rank	Name	Number of grants	Notes
32	Microsoft Corporation Contributions Program	72	
33	Western Union Foundation	72	
34	The Astraea Lesbian Foundation for Justice, Inc.	62	
35	The Kresge Foundation	60	PHEA
36	Howard G. Buffett Foundation	59	
37	Virginia Gildersleeve International Fund	59	
38	Public Welfare Foundation, Inc.	53	
39	EMpower—The Emerging Markets Foundation	48	

Grants made between 2003 and 2013 (Source: Foundation Center)

APPENDIX D

Table A.4 Top US Foundations grant recipients by country and linguistic groups—all sectors included

Commonwealth		Francophonie		Arab League	
Country	Total	Country	Total	Country	Total
South Africa	$1,163,607,934	Ghana	$156,604,359	Egypt	$76,968,172
Kenya	$1,140,091,091	Senegal	$91,737,887	Tunisia	$21,242,975
Nigeria	$361,595,257	Egypt	$76,968,172	Morocco	$5,258,793
Uganda	$195,968,970	Mauritius	$38,725,720	Sudan	$2,751,335
Ghana	$156,604,359	Mozambique	$38,714,429	Algeria	$559,876
Tanzania	$106,705,983	Tunisia	$21,242,975	Somalia	$465,406
Swaziland	$78,293,737	Burkina Faso	$20,783,750	Mauritania	$349,013
Zimbabwe	$70,783,757	Mali	$19,958,360	Libya	$309,215
Mauritius	$38,725,720	Rwanda	$18,250,044	Djibouti	$89,781
Mozambique	$38,714,429	Benin	$9,846,885	**TOTAL**	**$107,994,566**
Botswana	$24,073,160	Madagascar	$9,504,881		
Rwanda	$18,250,044	Congo DRC	$5,987,489		
Gambia, The	$16,593,994	Morocco	$5,258,793		
Zambia	$16,288,237	Cameroon	$4,717,709		
Lesotho	$15,719,521	Cote d'Ivoire	$3,193,716		
Malawi	$15,044,200	Guinea	$3,188,030		
Sierra Leone	$11,960,510	Burundi	$2,173,918		
Namibia	$10,666,509	Niger	$2,170,095		
Cameroon	$4,717,709	Chad	$967,412		
TOTAL	**$3,484,405,121**	Togo	$842,913		
		Gabon	$615,910		
		Guinea-Bissau	$161,927		
		Djibouti	$89,781		
		Equatorial Guinea	$30,300		
		Central African Rep.	$27,804		
		TOTAL	**$531,763,262**		

Grants made between 2003 and 2013 (Source: Foundation Center)

© The Editor(s) (if applicable) and The Author(s) 2016
F. Jaumont, *Unequal Partners*, Philanthropy and Education,
DOI 10.1057/978-1-137-59348-1

Appendix E

Table A.5 Top 50 higher education grant recipients of US foundations in Africa

Top grant recipients	Country	Total amount	Grants	Donors	Main donor(s)
University of Cape Town	South Africa	$124,308,789	275	23	Mellon, Gates, Carnegie
Coca-Cola Africa Foundation Scholarship Fund	Swaziland	$68,063,930	11	1	Coca-Cola Foundation.
University of the Western Cape	South Africa	$58,180,764	90	11	Atlantic Philanthropies, Ford, Kresge
University of the Witwatersrand	South Africa	$57,356,697	114	17	Mellon, Gates, Carnegie
Makerere University	Uganda	$52,161,802	91	11	Rockefeller, Carnegie, Gates
African Population and Health Research Center	Kenya	$43,677,571	59	8	Hewlett, Packard, Rockefeller
Regional Universities Forum for Capacity Building in Agriculture	Uganda	$40,436,883	17	4	Gates, Rockefeller, Carnegie
University of Pretoria	South Africa	$24,726,566	58	11	Carnegie, Gates, Kellogg
University of Ghana	Ghana	$24,697,338	29	8	Carnegie, Gates, Hewlett
University of KwaZulu-Natal	South Africa	$23,673,970	76	9	Rockefeller, Carnegie, Ford
TrustAfrica	Senegal	$22,704,568	19	9	Ford, Gates, Carnegie
University of Zimbabwe	Zimbabwe	$21,209,372	17	2	Kellogg, Rockefeller
Rhodes University	South Africa	$19,847,773	50	10	Mellon, Atlantic Philanthropies, Ford
International Livestock Research Institute	Kenya	$17,488,261	20	5	Gates, Rockefeller, Ford

(*continued*)

© The Editor(s) (if applicable) and The Author(s) 2016
F. Jaumont, *Unequal Partners*, Philanthropy and Education,
DOI 10.1057/978-1-137-59348-1

Table A.5   (continued)

Top grant recipients	Country	Total amount	Grants	Donors	Main donor(s)
South African Institute for Advancement	South Africa	$17,131,646	46	8	Kresge, Atlantic Philanthropies, Stewart Mott
University of Ibadan	Nigeria	$16,026,780	14	2	MacArthur, Ford
American University in Cairo	Egypt	$15,147,715	61	11	Ford, UN Women's Fund for Gender Equality, Open Society Institute
University of Dar es Salaam	Tanzania	$14,684,902	20	6	Carnegie, Ford, Rockefeller
University of Stellenbosch	South Africa	$12,591,192	43	16	Mellon, Gates, Ford
South African Institute for Distance Education	South Africa	$12,520,089	19	9	Hewlett, Ford, Carnegie
University of KwaZulu-Natal Foundation	South Africa	$11,550,491	9	1	Atlantic Philanthropies
Ahmadu Bello University	Nigeria	$10,042,618	13	4	MacArthur, Carnegie, Packard
Cheikh Anta Diop University	Senegal	$9,484,360	12	5	Gates, Hewlett, Bristol-Myers Squibb.
African Virtual University	Kenya	$9,399,744	10	6	Hewlett, Ford, MacArthur
Human Sciences Research Council	South Africa	$8,346,681	40	11	Gates, Ford, Hilton
Bayero University	Nigeria	$8,345,890	7	1	MacArthur
Obafemi Awolowo University	Nigeria	$8,188,235	4	2	Carnegie, Tides
Forum for African Women Educationalists	Kenya	$7,943,457	29	7	Rockefeller, Packard, Bristol-Myers Squibb
Cairo University	Egypt	$7,605,450	28	3	Ford, Avon, Mellon
University of Witwatersrand	South Africa	$7,507,129	12	2	Atlantic Philanthropies, Getty Trust
University of Jos	Nigeria	$7,472,500	4	1	Carnegie
University of the Free State	South Africa	$7,390,432	17	6	Kresge, Kellogg, Rockefeller
Nigeria ICT Forum of Partnership Institutions	Nigeria	$6,559,000	12	6	Carnegie, Ford, MacArthur
Development Association City Campus	South Africa	$6,198,280	12	5	Kellogg, Rockefeller, JPMorgan Chase
CHET	South Africa	$6,057,372	27	4	Ford, Carnegie, The Kresge
University of Port Harcourt	Nigeria	$5,085,200	6	2	MacArthur, Ford
Sokoine University of Agriculture	Tanzania	$4,939,029	15	5	Rockefeller, McKnight, Ford
University of Malawi	Malawi	$4,206,303	15	3	Rockefeller, McKnight, Carnegie
University of Nairobi	Kenya	$4,162,238	25	6	Ford, Rockefeller, McKnight

(continued)

Table A.5   (continued)

Top grant recipients	Country	Total amount	Grants	Donors	Main donor(s)
Pan-Atlantic University	Nigeria	$4,034,582	8	3	Goldman Sachs, Clover, Rockefeller
Tertiary Education Network	South Africa	$3,999,366	7	6	Mellon, Google.org, MacArthur
National University of Science and Technology	Zimbabwe	$3,898,509	3	1	Kellogg
Egerton University	Kenya	$3,835,230	15	3	Rockefeller, Gates, Ford
Nelson Mandela Metropolitan University	South Africa	$3,749,571	9	4	Atlantic Philanthropies, Ford, Kellogg
Ministry of Education of South Africa	South Africa	$3,668,848	1	1	Carnegie
Africa University	Zimbabwe	$3,612,232	13	5	Kellogg, Caterpillar, Magee Christian
University of Fort Hare	South Africa	$3,474,850	18	5	Kellogg, Ford, Mellon
Jomo Kenyatta University of Agriculture and Technology	Kenya	$3,301,327	15	5	Rockefeller, Gates, Conservation, Food and Health Foundation
University of South Africa	South Africa	$3,244,155	10	5	Kellogg, Gates, Ford
University of Bamako	Mali	$2,987,906	1	1	Gates

Grants made between 2003 and 2013 (Source: Foundation Center)

Appendix F

Table A.6 List of all US foundations and their higher education recipients in Africa

Grantmaker	State	Recipients and number of grants received (n)
Alcoa Foundation	PA	Africa University (1)
Alfred P. Sloan Foundation	NY	University of Cape Town (3), Bibliotheca Alexandrina (1)
Allen Foundation, Inc.	MI	University of Botswana (2)
Annenberg Foundation	CA	School of African Heritage (1)
Avon Foundation for Women	NY	Cairo University (1)
Banyan Tree Foundation	DC	Valley Trust (2), Forum for African Women Educationalists (2), Rhodes University (1)
Bill & Melinda Gates Foundation	WA	University of Cape Town (17) International Livestock Research Institute (5) University of Stellenbosch (5) Makerere University (5) Human Sciences Research Council (5) University of Eastern Africa, Baraton (3) Regional Universities Forum for Capacity Building in Agriculture (3) University of the Witwatersrand (3) University of Ghana (3) University of Pretoria (3) Egerton University (3) Cheikh Anta Diop University (3) Jomo Kenyatta University of Agriculture and Technology (2) University of Nairobi (2) Rhodes University (2) University of South Africa (2) Information Training and Outreach Centre for Africa (2) United States International University (2) University of KwaZulu-Natal (2) TrustAfrica (1), Tshwane University of Technology (1)

(continued)

© The Editor(s) (if applicable) and The Author(s) 2016
F. Jaumont, *Unequal Partners*, Philanthropy and Education,
DOI 10.1057/978-1-137-59348-1

Table A.6 (continued)

Grantmaker	State	Recipients and number of grants received (n)
Carnegie Corporation of New York	NY	University of Bamako (1), University of Dar es Salaam (1) University of Limpopo (1), American University in Cairo (1) Power-Free Education and Technology (1) South African Institute for Distance Education (1) African Virtual University (1), Ahmadu Bello University (1) Daystar University (1), Eduardo Mondlane University (1) University of Cape Town (25), Association of African Universities (17), Makerere University (13), University of the Witwatersrand (9), University of KwaZulu-Natal (8), University of Ghana (8), University of Pretoria (6), Centre for Higher Education Transformation Trust (6), University of Dar es Salaam (6), National Council for Tertiary Education (5), University of Jos (4), Nigeria ICT Forum of Partnership Institutions (4), South African Institute for Advancement (3), Obafemi Awolowo University (3), University of the Western Cape (3), University of Stellenbosch (3), TrustAfrica (2), African Population and Health Research Center (2), Bibliotheca Alexandrina (2), University for Development Studies (2), African Network of Scientific and Technological Institutions (2), Council for the Development of Social Science Research in Africa (2), Evaluation Research Agency (2), University World News (2), Ahmadu Bello University (1), Cape Higher Education Consortium (1), National Council for Higher Education (1), South African Institute for Distance Education (1), Tanzania Commission for Universities (1), Rhodes University (1), University of Fort Hare (1), African Virtual University (1), Human Sciences Research Council (1), Ministry of Education of South Africa (1), University of Malawi (1), Tertiary Education Network (1), Council on Higher Education (1), Higher Education South Africa (1), Southern African Research and Innovation Management Association (1), Regional Universities Forum for Capacity Building in Agriculture (1)
Carrie Estelle Doheny Foundation	CA	Maryvale College (1)
Caterpillar Foundation	IL	Africa University (2)
Channel Foundation	WA	Mbarara University of Science and Technology (1)
Charles Stewart Mott Foundation	MI	South African Institute for Advancement (10), University of the Western Cape (9), University of KwaZulu-Natal (8), Community Development Resource Association (7), University of Fort Hare (5), University of Cape Town (4), Participative Development Initiative (4), Rhodes University (4), Institute for Justice and Reconciliation (4), Human Sciences Research Council (4), Nelson Mandela Metropolitan University (3), University of South Africa (2), South African History Archive Trust (1), Khanya College Johannesburg Trust (1), University of the Witwatersrand (1), University of Port Elizabeth (1)
Citi Foundation	NY	American University in Cairo (6), HOPE Worldwide (4)
Clover Foundation	NY	Pan-Atlantic University (1)
Conrad N. Hilton Foundation	CA	Human Sciences Research Council (1)
Conservation, Food and Health Foundation, Inc.	MA	Jomo Kenyatta University of Agriculture and Technology (1)

(continued)

Grantmaker	State	Recipients and number of grants received (n)
CS Fund	CA	University of Cape Coast (1)
Disability Rights Fund	MA	Action for Youth with Disabilities Uganda (5)
Doris Duke Charitable Foundation	NY	University of Cape Town (3), African Population and Health Research Center (1)
Educational Pathways International	NV	University of Ghana (1)
Elaine and Donald Levinson Foundation	IL	University of the Witwatersrand (1)
EMpower—The Emerging Markets Foundation	NY	Equal Education (2)
Engineering Information Foundation	NY	Jomo Kenyatta University of Agriculture and Technology (1), University of Botswana (1), Eduardo Mondlane University (1), Headstart College (1)
Ernest E. and Brendalyn Stempel Foundation	NY	University of Cape Town (1)
Firelight Endowment	CA	Human Sciences Research Council (1)
Flora Family Foundation	CA	University of the Witwatersrand (2), Makerere University (1), African Population and Health Research Center (1), University of Stellenbosch (1), Valley Trust (1)
Ford Foundation Ford Foundation (continued)	NY	University of Cape Town (44), American University in Cairo (36), University of the Western Cape (29), University of the Witwatersrand (38), University of KwaZulu-Natal (30), Cairo University (26), Centre for Higher Education Transformation Trust (19), African Woman and Child Feature Service (15), Makerere University (14), University of Pretoria (14), University of Nairobi (12), Human Sciences Research Council (11), Rhodes University (10), University of Stellenbosch (9), African Population and Health Research Center (8), South African Institute for Advancement (8), Association of African Universities (7), University of Dar es Salaam (6), TrustAfrica (6), South African Institute for Distance Education (6), Council for the Development of Social Science Research in Africa (5), Equal Education (5), Association for Advancement of Higher Education & Development (5), Economic Research Forum for the Arab Countries, Iran and Turkey (5), Partners in Development for Research, Consulting and Training (5), Catholic University of Mozambique (4), Cabinet Information and Decision Support Center (4), Assiut University (4), Cape Higher Education Consortium (4), National Egyptian Fertility Care Foundation (4), University of the North (4), University of Fort Hare (4), Bibliotheca Alexandrina (4), University of the Free State (3), University of Ghana (3), Nelson Mandela Metropolitan University (3), University of South Africa (3), Higher Education South Africa (3), University of Namibia (3), Students and Youth Working on Reproductive Health-Action Team (3), Elgin Learning Foundation (3), United Nations Economic Commission for Africa (3), University of Venda (3), Strathmore University (3), AfriHUB Nigeria (3), Free State Higher Education Consortium Trust (3), Foundation of

(continued)

Table A.6   (continued)

Grantmaker	State	Recipients and number of grants received (n)
		Tertiary Institutions in the Northern Metropolis (3), University of Johannesburg (3), Mozambique, Republic of (3), Council on Higher Education (3), Workers College (3), Valley Trust (2), Institute for Justice and Reconciliation (2), Higher Education Loans Board (2), Kenya Education Network Trust (2), Ministry of Higher Education, Science and Technology (2), Academy of Science of South Africa (2), Dreamers of Tomorrow Association (2), University World News (2), Eduardo Mondlane University (2), Kenyatta University (2), South African History Archive Trust (2), Women Educational Researchers of Kenya (2), National Library and Archives of Egypt (2), American University in Cairo (2), Regional Universities Forum for Capacity Building in Agriculture (2), International Livestock Research Institute (2), Egerton University (2), Sokoine University of Agriculture (2), Walter Sisulu University for Technology and Science (2), Nigeria ICT Forum of Partnership Institutions (2), University of Port Harcourt (1), African Network Operators Group (1), University of North-West (1), Committee of Vice-Chancellors of Nigerian Federal Universities (1), Nigerian Publishers Association (1), Applied Social Science Forum (1), Centre for Management Development (1), International Centre for Mathematical and Computer Sciences (1), Zimbabwe College of Music (1), Ecole Superieure des Arts Visuels Marrakech (1), University of Ibadan (1), African Virtual University (1), Association Marocaine de Lutte Contre le SIDA (1), Southern African Wildlife College (1), SCEZONS CC (1), Nairobi Peace Initiative-Africa (1), Youth Dreamers of Tomorrow (1), Inter-University Council for East Africa (1), Sizanang Centre for Research and Development (1), Suez Canal University (1), Endowment Consortium Foundation (1), Ministry of Higher Education (1), Quality Experts Group (1), University of Minia (1), University of Limpopo (1),Monash Educational Enterprises (1), Mkuki na Nyota Publishers (1), University of Port Elizabeth (1), National Access Consortium of the
Foundation to Promote Open Society	NY	Western Cape Trust (1) University of Stellenbosch (1), Equal Education (1), University of the Western Cape (1).
Fund For Global Human Rights, Inc.	DC	Association Marocaine de Lutte Contre le SIDA (2)
GE Foundation	CT	University of Namibia Foundation (2)
Gilead Foundation	CA	Eduardo Mondlane University (1)
Global Greengrants Fund	CO	University of Botswana (1)
Google.org	CA	Nigeria ICT Forum of Partnership Institutions (1), Tertiary Education Network (1)
Harry J. Lloyd Charitable Trust	KS	Kenya Highlands Bible College (1)
Humanity United	CA	TrustAfrica (1)
International Christian Scholarship Foundation	CA	Daystar University (1)

(*continued*)

Grantmaker	State	Recipients and number of grants received (n)
J. Paul Getty Trust	CA	School of African Heritage (3), American University in Cairo (1), University of the Witwatersrand Foundation (1)
James S. McDonnell Foundation	MO	University of Cape Town (3)
John M. Lloyd Foundation	CA	University of the Witwatersrand (1)
John Templeton Foundation	PA	University of Ouagadougou (1)
Johnson & Johnson Family of Companies Foundation	NJ	American University in Cairo (1)
King Baudouin Foundation United States, Inc.	NY	South African Institute for Advancement (1), Cape Peninsula University of Technology (1)
Koch Foundation, Inc.	FL	Saint Viator College (1)
Levi Strauss Foundation	CA	University of Nairobi (2)
Magee Christian Education Foundation	OH	Africa University (2)
Marin Community Foundation	CA	University of Cape Coast (4)
Microsoft Corporation Contributions Program	WA	South African Institute for Distance Education (1), Tertiary Education Network (1), Khanya College Johannesburg Trust (1)
Motorola Solutions Foundation	IL	Community and Individual Development Association City Campus (2), ABTI-American University of Nigeria (1), Central Johannesburg College (1), University of Cape Town (1), University of Stellenbosch (1)
Mustard Seed Foundation, Inc.	VA	Africa International University (6), University of Stellenbosch (1), Daystar University (1), Uganda Christian University (1)
National Endowment for Democracy	DC	Applied Social Science Forum (1)
Omidyar Network Fund, Inc.	CA	Shehu Musa Yaradua Foundation (1)
Open Society Institute	NY	American University in Cairo (4), Equal Education (2), Applied Social Science Forum (2), University of the Western Cape (2), Makerere University (2), University of Pretoria (2), University of Stellenbosch (1), Council for the Development of Social Science Research in Africa (1)
Oscar C. Rixson Foundation, Inc.	NC	Daystar University (1)
Raskob Foundation for Catholic Activities, Inc.	DE	Diocese of Makurdi (1)
Robertson Foundation	NY	University of Ghana (3)
Rockefeller Brothers Fund, Inc.	NY	University of Cape Town (14), Human Sciences Research Council (6), University of the Western Cape (4), University of KwaZulu-Natal (4), University of the Witwatersrand (2), Tomorrow Trust (2) Rhodes University (1), Bibliotheca Alexandrina (1)
Royce Family Fund, Inc.	CT	Uganda Christian University (2)
Silicon Valley Community Foundation	CA	Makerere University (1), Community and Individual Development Association City Campus (1)

(continued)

Table A.6   (continued)

Grantmaker	State	Recipients and number of grants received (n)
State Street Foundation, Inc.	MA	Southern African Wildlife College (1), New Africa Theatre Association (1)
Suissa Charitable Fund, Inc.	IL	University of the Witwatersrand (1)
The Andrew W. Mellon Foundation	NY	University of Cape Town (97), University of the Witwatersrand (39), Rhodes University (22), University of the Western Cape (15), University of KwaZulu-Natal (9), University of Stellenbosch (7), University of Fort Hare (6), University of Pretoria (5), Cape Higher Education Consortium (5), Foundation of Tertiary Institutions in the Northern Metropolis (3), University of Ghana (2), University of the Free State (2), Tertiary Education Network (2), Makerere University (2), Eastern Seaboard Association of Tertiary Institutions Trust (2), Higher Education South Africa (1), New Africa Theatre Association (1), Universite Mohammed V Agdal (1), Cairo University (1), University of South Africa (1)
The Atlantic Philanthropies	NY	University of Cape Town (14), University of the Western Cape (14), University of the Witwatersrand Foundation (11), University of KwaZulu-Natal Foundation (9), South African Institute for Advancement (8), Rhodes University (6), Human Sciences Research Council (3), Nelson Mandela Metropolitan University (2), Walter Sisulu University for Technology and Science (2), Durban University of Technology (2), Institute for Justice and Reconciliation (1), South African History Archive Trust (1)
The Bodman Foundation	NY	American University in Cairo (2)
The Bristol-Myers Squibb Foundation, Inc.	NY	Human Sciences Research Council (5), Forum for African Women Educationalists (4), Cheikh Anta Diop University (4), National University of Lesotho (4), University of Namibia (2), University of Swaziland (2), Fond National Pour L'Education et La Recherche (2) Association Marocaine de Lutte Contre le SIDA (1), University of Lubumbashi (1), Valley Trust (1)
The Charles A. Dana Foundation, Inc.	NY	University of Cape Town (1), Ain Shams University (1)
The Christensen Fund	CA	Hawassa University (2), Arba Minch University (2), Mizan-Tepi University (1), Addis Ababa University (1)
The Coca-Cola Foundation, Inc.	GA	Coca-Cola Africa Foundation (11)
The Community Foundation for Greater Atlanta	GA	Africa University (1)
The David and Lucile Packard Foundation	CA	African Population and Health Research Center (10), Addis Ababa University (2), TrustAfrica (1), Ahmadu Bello University (1), Forum for African Women Educationalists (2), YWCA of Ethiopia (1)
The Four P Foundation	TX	Uganda Christian University (1)
The Global Fund for Women	CA	University of Dar es Salaam (1), Forum for African Women Educationalists (1), African Woman and Child Feature Service (1), Headstart College (1)

Grantmaker	State	Recipients and number of grants received (n)
The Goldman Sachs Foundation	NY	Pan-Atlantic University (6), University of Pretoria (2), United States International University, (2)University of Dar es Salaam (1),
The Harry Frank Guggenheim Foundation	NY	Afrika Study Center (2)
The J.W. Foundation	NY	TrustAfrica (1)
The John D. and Catherine T. MacArthur Foundation	IL	University of Ibadan (13), Ahmadu Bello University (10), Bayero University (7), University of Antananarivo (6), Makerere University (4), University of Port Harcourt (5), Nigeria ICT Forum of Partnership Institutions (3), National University of Rwanda (3), TrustAfrica (3), Shehu Musa Yaradua Foundation (3), Committee of Vice-Chancellors of Nigerian Federal Universities (2), National Universities Commission (2), Mbarara University of Science and Technology (2), University of the Witwatersrand (2), Federal Ministry of Education (2), National Commission for Colleges of Education (2), ABTI-American University of Nigeria (1), Universite de Toliara (1), African Virtual University (1), African Network Operators Group (1), University of Cape Town (1), South African Institute for Distance Education (1), Cheikh Anta Diop University (1), University of Botswana (1), Tertiary Education Network (1), Sokoine University of Agriculture (1), University of Pretoria (1), University of Benin (1), Federal University of Technology, Minna (1), Machina Emirate Development Association (1)
The JPMorgan Chase Foundation	NY	Development Association City Campus (3), South African Institute for Advancement (1), Community and Individual
The Judy & Howard Berkowitz Foundation	NY	University of Stellenbosch (1)
The Kresge Foundation	MI	South African Institute for Advancement (14), University of the Western Cape (8), University of the Witwatersrand (6), Cape Peninsula University of Technology (6), University of Pretoria (7), University of the Free State (4), Rhodes University (2), University of Stellenbosch (1), South African Institute for Distance Education (1), Centre for Higher Education Transformation Trust (1), Durban University of Technology (1), University of Johannesburg (1), Tswhane University of Technology (1), University of Cape Town (1)
The Lois and George Castrucci Family Foundation	FL	Kenya Education Network Trust (1)
The McKnight Foundation	MN	University of Malawi (8), Makerere University (6), Sokoine University of Agriculture (4), International Livestock Research Institute (1), University of Nairobi (1), Moi University (1), University of Ouagadougou (1)
The Medtronic Foundation	MN	University of Stellenbosch (1)
The Michael and Susan Dell Foundation	TX	University of Cape Town (20), University of Pretoria (7), University of Stellenbosch (2), University of the Free State (1)
The New York Community Trust	NY	University of Stellenbosch (3)

(continued)

Table A.6 (continued)

Grantmaker	State	Recipients and number of grants received (n)
The Overbrook Foundation	NY	University of Cape Town (1), South African Institute for Advancement (1)
The Patricia William Mwangaza Foundation, Inc.	NC	Jomo Kenyatta University of Agriculture and Technology (1), Daystar University (1)
The Pittsburgh Foundation	PA	Sokoine University of Agriculture (1)
The Rockefeller Foundation	NY	Makerere University (41), Forum for African Women Educationalists (13), University of Cape Town (12), African Population and Health Research Center (11), Regional Universities Forum for Capacity Building in Agriculture (11), University of KwaZulu-Natal (11), International Livestock Research Institute (11), Egerton University (10), Jomo Kenyatta University of Agriculture and Technology (10), University of Zimbabwe (8), Sokoine University of Agriculture (7), University of Nairobi (7), University of Pretoria (8), Association of African Universities (6), University of Malawi (6), Moi University (6), University of Dar es Salaam (5), University of Ghana (4), University of Stellenbosch (4), University of the Western Cape (4), National Council for Higher Education (3), Kenya Education Network Trust (3), University of the Free State (3), University of Zambia (3), National University of Rwanda (3), United Nations Economic Commission for Africa (2), Association City Campus (2), Strathmore University (2), Kenyatta University (2), Cape Higher Education Consortium (2), South African Institute for Distance Education (1), Cheikh Anta Diop University (1), African Virtual University (1), Nigeria ICT Forum of Partnership Institutions (1), Community and Individual Development Centre for Higher Education Transformation Trust (1), Pan-Atlantic University (1), University of the Witwatersrand (1), Tertiary Education Network (1), Council for the Development of Social Science Research in Africa (1), Information Training and Outreach Centre for Africa (1), Catholic University of Mozambique (1), University of Ouagadougou (1), Association for the Advancement of Higher Education and Development (1), University of Botswana (1), Mbarara University of Science and Technology (1), Kigali Institute of Science and Technology (1), African Network Operators Group (1), Mekelle University (1), University of Liberia (1), University for Development Studies (1), Open University of Tanzania (1)
The Spencer Foundation	IL	University of Cape Town (2), University of KwaZulu-Natal (2), University of the Western Cape (1), University of the Witwatersrand (1), Human Sciences Research Council (1), University of Benin (1)

(continued)

Table A.6   (continued)

Grantmaker	State	Recipients and number of grants received (n)
The Starr Foundation	NY	Loyola Jesuit College (4)
The William and Flora Hewlett Foundation	CA	University of Cape Town (6), University of the Witwatersrand (5), African Population and Health Research Center (23), University of Ghana (5), African Virtual University (5), American University in Cairo (4), South African Institute for Distance Education (6), Cheikh Anta Diop University (3), University of Mauritius (2), Women Educational Researchers of Kenya (2), University of Nairobi (1), University of Ouagadougou (1), University of Cape Coast (1), Meraka Institute (1), Rhodes University (1)
Tides Foundation	CA	African Women Educationalists (6), Action for Youth with Disabilities Uganda (2), Makerere University (2), University of Cape Town (1), University of the Witwatersrand (1), Obafemi Awolowo University (1), Forum for Nigeria ICT Forum of Partnership Institutions (1), Kenyatta University (1),
UN Women's Fund for Gender Equality	NY	American University in Cairo (1)
Virginia Gildersleeve International Fund	NY	Forum for African Women Educationalists (1)
W. K. Kellogg Foundation	MI	University of Zimbabwe (9), Africa University (7), University of the Free State (4), National University of Lesotho (4), Community and Individual Development Association City Campus (4), National University of Science and Technology (3), University of Cape Town (3), University of Pretoria (3), University of KwaZulu-Natal (2), University of Fort Hare (2), University of South Africa (2), University of Stellenbosch (2), Human Sciences Research Council (2), CIDA City Campus (2), HOPE Worldwide (2), Valley Trust (2), South African Institute for Distance Education (1), Nelson Mandela Metropolitan University (1), International Livestock Research Institute (1), Instituto Superior Politecnico de Manica (1), Tshwane University of Technology (1), University of the Witwatersrand (1), TrustAfrica (1), Catholic University of Mozambique (1), Institute for Justice and Reconciliation (1), University of Venda (1), University of Botswana (1), University of Swaziland (1), BOOST Fellowship (1), Ba Isago University College (1), Zimbabwe Open University (1), Women's University in Africa (1)
Wallace Global Fund II	DC	TrustAfrica (3), Equal Education (2)University of Cape Town (1)
Western Union Foundation	CO	American University in Cairo (3), University of Namibia Foundation (1)
Wikimedia Foundation, Inc.	CA	Information Training and Outreach Centre for Africa (1)

Grants made between 2003 and 2013 (Source: Foundation Center)

BIBLIOGRAPHY

Adam, Thomas. 2004. *Philanthropy, patronage, and civil society. Experiences from Germany, Great Britain, and North America.* Bloomington: Indiana University Press.

Akst, Daniel. 2004. What are foundations for? *Carnegie Reporter* 3(1). Carnegie Corporation of New York.

Allen, T., and A. Thomas. 2000. *Agencies of development in poverty and development into the 21st century.* Oxford: The Open University.

Amutabi, Maurice N. 2013. *The NGO factor in Africa: The case of arrested development in Kenya.* New York: Routledge.

Anheier, Helmut K., and David C. Hammack. 2010. *American foundations: Roles and contributions.* Washington, DC: The Brookings Institution.

Anheier, Helmut K., and Stefan Toepler. 1999. *Private funds, public purpose philanthropic foundations in international perspective.* New York: Kluwer/Plenum Publishers.

Archibald, M. 2004. Between isomorphism and market partitioning: How organizational competencies and resources foster cultural and sociopolitical legitimacy, and promote organizational survival. In *Research in the sociology of organizations*, ed. C. Johnson, 171–211. London: Emerald.

Ashforth, Blake E., and Barrie W. Gibbs. 1990. The double-edge of organizational legitimation. *Organization Science* 1(2): 177–194.

Astin, Alexander, and Astin Helen. 2000. *Leadership reconsidered: Engaging higher education in social change.* Detroit: W.K. Kellogg Foundation.

Atieno-Odhiambo, E.S. 2000. Africa's place in world dialogue at the beginning of the 21st century. In *Africa at the beginning of the 21st century*, ed. G.P. Okoth. Nairobi: Nairobi University Press.

Banya, Kingsley, and Juliet Elu. 2001. The world bank and financing higher education in sub-Saharan Africa. *Higher Education* 42(1): 1–34.

Berman, Edward H. 1977. American philanthropy and African education: Toward an analysis. *African Studies Review* 20(1): 71–85.

Berman, Edward H. 1978. Review: The foundations' interest in Africa. *History of Education Quarterly* 18(4): 461–470.

Bertelsmann Foundation (ed.). 1999. *The future of foundations in an open society.* Gütersloh: Bertelsmann Foundation Publishers.

© The Editor(s) (if applicable) and The Author(s) 2016
F. Jaumont, *Unequal Partners*, Philanthropy and Education,
DOI 10.1057/978-1-137-59348-1

Bremner, Robert H. 2000. *American philanthropy*. Chicago: The University of Chicago Press. 1988.

Bremner, Robert H. 1994. *Giving. Charity and philanthropy in history*. New Brunswick: Transaction Publishers.

Brinkerhoff, Derick W. 1986. The evolution of current perspectives on institutional development: An organizational focus. In *Politics, projects, and people: Institutional development in Haiti*, ed. Derick W. Brinkerhoff and Jean-Claude Garcia-Zamor, 11–62. New York: Praeger Publishers.

Buchanan, Bob, and Booker Jayne. 2007. *Making a difference in Africa: Advice from experienced grantmakers*. Washington, DC: Council on Foundations and Africa Grantmakers'Affinity Group.

Bullock, Mary B. 1980. *An American transplant: The Rockefeller foundation and Peking Union Medical College*. Berkeley/Los Angeles: University of California Press.

Burnell, Peter. 2001. *Foreign aid in a changing world*. Buckingham/Philadelphia: Open University Press.

Butler, Lorna Michael, and Della E. McMillan (eds.). 2015. *Tapping philanthropy for development: Lessons learned from a public-private partnership in rural Uganda*. Boulder: Kumarian Press.

Calderisi, Robert. 2006. *The trouble with Africa: Why foreign aid isn't working*. New York: Palgrave MacMillan.

Cascione, Gregory L. 2003. *Philanthropists in higher education institutional, biographical, and religious motivations for giving*. New York: Routledge.

Cloete, Nico, Tracy Bailey, Pundy Pillay, Ian Bunting, and Peter Maassen. 2011. *Universities and economic development in Africa*. Wynberg: CHET.

Condliffe Lagemann, Ellen. 1999. *Philanthropic foundations. New scholarship, new possibilities*. Bloomington: Indiana University Press.

Conley, Darlene Joy. 1990. *Philanthropic foundations and organizational change: The case of the Southern education foundation (SEF) during the civil rights era*. Doctoral dissertation, Northwestern University.

Cooksey, Brian, Daniel Mkube, and Lisbeth Levey. 2003. *Higher education in Tanzania. Partnership for Higher Education in Africa*. Oxford: James Currey.

Coombe, Trevor. 1991. *A consultation on higher education in Africa. A report to the ford foundation and the Rockefeller foundation*. University of London.

Coon, Horace. 1990. *Money to burn. Great American foundations and their money*. Originally published in 1938 by Longmans, Green, and Co. New Brunswick: Transaction Publishers.

Cueto, Marcos. 1994a. Visions of science and development: Rockefeller foundation's Latin American surveys of the 1920s. In *Missionaries of science: The Rockefeller foundation in Latin America*, ed. Marcos Cueto. Bloomington/Indianapolis: Indiana University Press.

Cueto, Marcos (ed.). 1994b. *Missionaries of science: The Rockefeller foundation in Latin America*. Bloomington/Indianapolis: Indiana University Press.

Damon, William, and Susan Verducci. 2006. *Taking philanthropy seriously: Beyond noble intentions to responsible giving*. Bloomington: Indiana University Press.

Dichter, T. 1997. Appeasing the gods of sustainability. In *NGOs, states and donors*, ed. D. Hulme and M. Edwards. London: MacMillan.

DiMaggio, Paul. 1982. Cultural entrepreneurship in nineteenth-century Boston. *Media, Culture and Society* 4 : 33–50.

DiMaggio, Paul. 1988. Interest and agency in institutional theory. In *Institutional patterns and organizations*, ed. L.G. Zucker, 3–22. Cambridge, MA: Ballinger.

DiMaggio, Paul J., and Walter W. Powell. 1983. The iron cage revisited: Institutional isomorphism and collective rationality in organizational fields. *American Sociological Review* 48: 147–160.

DiMaggio, Paul J., and Walter W. Powell. 1991. *The new institutionalism in organizational analysis*. Chicago: University of Chicago Press.

Edie, John A., and Jane C. Nober. 2002. *Beyond our borders: A guide to making grants outside of the United States*. Arlington: Council on Foundations.

Edwards, M., and D. Hulme. 1998. Too close for comfort? The impact of official aid on nongovernmental organization. *Current Issues in Comparative Education* 1(10): 1–32.

Fitzgerald, Deborah. 1994. Exporting American agriculture: Rockefeller foundation in Mexico, 1943–1953. In *Missionaries of science: The Rockefeller foundation in Latin America*, ed. Marcos Cueto. Bloomington/Indianapolis: Indiana University.

Fleishman, Joel, Scott Kohler, and Steven Schindler. 2007. *Casebook for the foundation: A great American secret; how private wealth is changing the world*. New York: Public Affairs.

Fosdick, Raymond B. 1989. *The story of the Rockefeller foundation*. New Brunswick: Transaction Publishers.

Fowler, Alan. 1988. *Non-governmental organizations in Africa: Achieving comparative advantage in relief and micro-development*. IDS Discussion Paper 249. Sussex: IDS Sussex.

Fowler, Alan. 1991. The role of NGOs in changing state-society relations: Perspectives from Eastern and Southern Africa. *Development Policy Review* 9(1): 53–84.

Fowler, Alan, P. Campbell, and B. Pratt. 1992. *Institutional development and NGOs in Africa: Policy perspectives for European development agencies*. Oxford: INTRAC.

Funders Concerned about AIDS. 2008. *Funder collaborations addressing HIV/AIDS: Examples from around the world*. A presentation of 19 case studies. New York, NY.

Gasman, Marybeth, and Katherine V. Sedgwick (eds.). 2005. *Uplifting a people: African American philanthropy and education*. New York: Peter Lang Publishing.

Gibbons, Michael. 1998. *Higher education relevance in the 21st century. Human development network*. Washington, DC: The World Bank.

Grant, Craft. 2009. *Funder collaboratives: Why and how funders work together*. New York, NY: Foundation Center.

Gray, Barbara. 1989. *Collaborating. Finding common ground for multiparty problems*. San Francisco: Jossey-Bass.

Gray, Barbara, and Donna J. Wood. 1991. Toward a comprehensive theory of collaboration. *The Journal of Applied Behavioral Science* 27(2): 139–162.

Greenwood, R., C. Oliver, R. Suddaby, and K. Sahlin. 2008. *Handbook of organizational institutionalism*. London: Sage.

Guilhot, Nicolas. 2004. Une Vocation Philanthropique, George Soros. Les Sciences Sociales et La Régulation du Marché Mondial. *Sociologie De La Mondialisation* N° 151–152/1–2.

Hancock, Graham. 1989. *Lords of poverty: The power, prestige and corruption of international aid business*. New York: Atlantic Monthly Press.

Hellinger, D. 1987. NGOs and the large aid donors: Changing the terms of development. *World Development* 15 (Special Supplement): 135–143.

Hess, Frederick M. 2005. *With the best of intentions: How philanthropy is reshaping K-12 education*. Cambridge: Harvard Education Press.

Hulme, David, and Michael Edwards (eds.). 1992. *Making a difference? NGOs and development in a changing world.* London: Earthscan.

Jaumont, Fabrice. 2014. *Strategic philanthropy, organizational legitimacy, and the development of higher education in Africa: The Partnership for Higher Education in Africa (2000–2010).* Doctoral Dissertation, New York University. ProQuest.

Jaumont, Fabrice. 2016. Dynamics of collaboration between U.S. foundations and African universities. In *Facilitating higher education growth through fundraising and philanthropy,* ed. H. Alphin, J. Lavine, S. Stark, and A. Hocker. Hershey: IGI Global.

Jaumont, Fabrice, and Jack Klempay. 2015. Measuring the influence of language on grantmaking by U.S. foundations in Africa. *Reconsidering Development* 4(1): 51–65.

Johnson, R. Burke, and Anthony J. Onwuegbuzie. 2004. Mixed methods research: A research paradigm whose time has come. *Educational Researcher* 33(7): 14–26.

Kanter, R.M. 1994. Collaborative advantage: The art of alliances. *Harvard Business Review* 72: 96–108.

Karin, Fisher, and Lindow Megan. 2008. Africa attracts renewed attention from American universities. *The Chronicle of Higher Education,* July 18.

Kemp, Amy. 2004. *The Rockefeller foundation and the Faculdade De Medicina De Sao Paulo: A case study in philanthropy as policy.* Doctoral dissertation, Indiana University.

Kovacs, Philip (ed.). 2011. *The gates foundation and the future of U.S. "public" schools.* New York: Routledge.

Kraatz, M.S., and E.J. Zajac. 1996. Exploring the limits of the new institutionalism: The causes and consequences of illegitimate organizational change. *American Sociological Review* 61: 812–836.

Leat, D., and H.K. Anheier. 2006. *Creative philanthropy: Toward a new philanthropy for the twenty-first century.* Los Angeles: University of California.

Lecours, André. 2005. *New institutionalism, theory, and analysis.* Toronto: University of Toronto Press.

Lewis, D. 2002. The rise of non-governmental organizations: Issues in development management. In *Handbook on development policy and management,* ed. C. Kirkpatrick, R. Clarke, and C. Polidano. New York: Edward Elgar Publishing.

March, James, and Johan P. Olsen. 1976. *Ambiguity and choice in organizations.* Bergen: Universitetsforlaget.

March, James, and Johan P. Olsen. 1989. *Rediscovering institutions. The organizational basis of politics.* New York: Free Press.

Masseys-Bertoneche, Carole. 2006. *Philanthropie et Grandes Universités Privées Américaines : Pouvoir et Réseaux d'Influence.* Bordeaux: Presses Universitaires de Bordeaux.

Mattessich, Paul W., Marta Murray-Close, and Barbara R. Monsey. 2001. *Collaboration: What makes it work.* Saint Paul: Fieldstone Alliance.

Meyer, John W., and Brian Rowan. 1977. Institutionalized organizations: Formal structure as myth and ceremony. *American Journal of Sociology* 83: 340–363.

Meyer, Heinz-Dieter, and Brian Rowan. 2006. *The new institutionalism in education.* Albany: State University of New York Press.

Meyer, John W., and Richard W. Scott. 1983. *Organizational environments: Ritual and rationality.* Beverly Hills: Sage.

Mike, Martin W. 1994. *Virtuous giving. Philanthropy, voluntary service, and caring.* Bloomingdale: Indiana University Press.

Mizruchi, M., and L.C. Fein. 1999. The social construction of organizational knowledge: A study of the uses of coercive, mimetic and normative isomorphism. *Administrative Science Quarterly* 44: 653–683.

Moja, Teboho. 2000. *A review of the ford foundation's impact on higher education in Africa*. New York University (Unpublished).

Moja, Teboho. 2006. *Internationalizing the curriculum. The internationalization of higher education in South Africa*. A publication of the International Education Association of South Africa.

Moja, Teboho. 2008. Politics of exclusion in higher education: the inadequacy of gender issues in the globalisation debates. In *Women and higher education in Africa: Reconceptualizing gender-based human capabilities and upgrading human rights to knowledge*, ed. N'Dri T. Assié-Lumumba. Abidjan: CEPARRED.

Murphy, Jefferson. 1976. *Carnegie corporation and Africa, 1953–1973*. New York: Teachers College Press.

Nelson, Paul J. 1995. *The World Bank and NGOs: The limits of apolitical development*. New York: St. Martins.

OECD. 2003. Philanthropic foundations and development co-operation. *The DAC Journal* 4(3): 73.

Okoth, Godfrey. 2000. Uganda's foreign economic relations from 1962 to the beginning of the twenty first century. In *Africa at the beginning of the 21st century*, ed. P.G. Okoth. Nairobi: Nairobi University Press.

Oliver, Christine. 1988. The collective strategy framework: An application to competing predictions of isomorphism. *Administrative Science Quarterly* 33: 543–561.

Osborn, D. 1993. *The west and development in Africa*. New York: Sage.

Osodo, P., and S. Matsvai. 1998. *Partners or contractors? The relationship between official agencies and NGOs: Kenya and Zimbabwe*, Occasional paper series, vol. 16. Oxford: The International NGO Training and Research Center (INTRAC). 62p.

Parmar, Inderjeet. 2004. *Selling Americanism, combatting anti-Americanism: The historical role of American foundations*. Hungary: Budapest. Center for Policy Studies, Central European University.

Payton, Robert L. 1988. *Philanthropy. Voluntary action for the public good*. New York: Macmillan.

Payton, Robert L., and Michael P. Moody. 2008. *Understanding philanthropy. Its meaning and mission*. Bloomington: Indiana University Press.

Person, Ann E., et al. 2009. *Maximizing the value of philanthropic efforts through planned partnerships between the U.S. government and private foundations*. Washington, DC: U.S. Department of Health and Human Services.

Pfeffer, Jeffrey, and Gerald Salancik. 1978. *The external control of organizations: A resource dependence perspective*. New York: Harper and Row.

Pfitzer, Marc, and Mike Stamp. 2010. *Multiplying impact through philanthropic collaboration*. A report for the European Foundation Centre. FSG Social Impact Advisors.

Phillips, N., T.B. Lawrence, and C. Hardy. 2000. Inter-organizational collaboration and the dynamics of institutional fields. *Journal of Management Studies* 37: 23–43.

Pifer, Alan. 2001. *Speaking out. Reflections on 30 years of foundation work*. Washington, DC: Council on Foundations.

Plastrik, P., and M. Taylor. 2004. *Network power for philanthropy and nonprofits*. Boston: Barr Foundation.

Powell, Walter W., and Elisabeth S. Clemens (eds.). 1998. *Private action and the public good*. New Haven: Yale University Press.

Prewitt, Kenneth. 1966. Makerere: Intelligence vs intellectuals. *Transition* 27: 35–39.

Raymond, Susan, and Mary Beth Martin. 2007. *Mapping the new world of American philanthropy, causes and consequences of the transfer of wealth*. Hoboken: Wiley.

Rockefeller, John D. 1983. The difficult art of giving. In *America's voluntary spirit. A book of readings*, ed. Brian O'Connell. New York: The Foundation Center.

Roelofs, Joan. 2007. Foundations and collaboration. *Critical Sociology* 33: 479.

Rosenfield, Patricia L. 2014. *A world of giving. Carnegie Corporation of New York. A Century of International Philanthropy*. New York: PublicAffairs.

Rossiter, Jenny, and Robin Palmer. 1990. Northern NGOs in Southern Africa: Some heretical thoughts, In *Critical choices for the NGO community: African development in the 1990s*, Seminar Proceedings No. 30. Proceedings of a conference held in the Center of African Studies, University of Edinburgh, 24 and 25 May 1990, p. 36.

Salamon, Lester M. 2002. *The state of nonprofit America*. Washington, DC: Brookings Institution Press.

Salamon, Lester M. 2003. *The state of nonprofit America*. Washington, DC: Brookings Institution Press.

Scott, Richard W. 1995. *Institutions and organizations*. Thousand Oaks: Sage.

Sears, Jesse B. 1990. *Philanthropy in the history of American higher education*. New Brunswick: Transaction Publishers.

Shaplen, Robert. 1964. *Toward the well-being of mankind: Fifty years of the Rockefeller foundation*. New York: Doubleday and Company.

Solorzano Ramos, Armando. 1990. *The Rockefeller foundation in Mexico: Nationalism, public health and yellow fever (1911–1924)*. Doctoral dissertation, The University of Wisconsin, Madison.

Srivastava, Prachi, and Su-Ann Oh. 2010. Private foundations, philanthropy, and partnership in education and development: Mapping the Terrain. *International Journal of Educational Development* 30: 460–471, 462.

St-Pierre, Danièle, and Lisa Burley. 2010. Factors influencing donor partnership effectiveness. *Foundation Review* 1: 4.

Suchman, Mark C. 1995. Managing legitimacy: Strategic and institutional approaches. *Academy of Management Review* 20: 571–610.

The World Bank. 2002. *Constructing knowledge societies: New challenges for tertiary education*. Washington, DC: The World Bank.

Thelin, John R., and Richard W. Trollinger. 2013. *Philanthropy and American higher education*. New York: Palgrave Macmillan.

Toepler, Stefan. 1998. Foundations and their institutional context: Cross-evaluating evidence from Germany and the United States. *Voluntas: International Journal of Voluntary and Nonprofit Organizations* 9(2): 153–170.

Whitaker, Ben. 1974a. *The foundations: An anatomy of philanthropic bodies*. New York: Penguin.

Whitaker, Ben. 1974b. *The philanthropoids. Foundations and society*. New York: Morrow.

Wiepking, Pamala, and Femida Handy. 2015. *The Palgrave handbook of global philanthropy*. New York: Palgrave Macmillan.

Zeleza, Paul Tiyambe. 2003. *Rethinking Africa's globalization: The intellectual challenge*. Trenton: Africa World Press.

Zurcher, Arnold J., and Jane Dustan. 1972. *The foundation administrator. A study of those who manage America's foundations*. New York: Russell Sage Foundation.

INDEX[1]

---

[1] Note: Page numbers with "n" denote notes.

© The Editor(s) (if applicable) and The Author(s) 2016

F. Jaumont, *Unequal Partners*, Philanthropy and Education,

DOI 10.1057/978-1-137-59348-1